Expect a Miracle!

If anyone had told us years ago that we would be helping other couples build "miracle marriages," we would have laughed. Our relationship looked hopeless.

But God took two of the most unlikely people and welded a bond that has given us immeasurable pleasure and security. We turned our hurtful pasts and damaged relationships into a marriage that glorifies Him. And every day our love grows deeper and more exciting.

That's not normal.

That's a miracle.

We encourage you to expect a miracle in your marriage. Our God is a master at taking broken pieces and creating whole, beautiful relationships. Allow Him to work, and you'll see.

—*Don and LaDean*

REMARRIED WITH CHILDREN

DON & LADEAN HOUCK

Here's Life Publishers

First Printing, October 1991

Published by
HERE'S LIFE PUBLISHERS, INC.
P. O. Box 1576
San Bernardino, CA 92402

Library of Congress Cataloging-in-Publication Data
Houck, Don.
  Re-married with children : a blended couple's journey to harmony /
Don and LaDean Houck.
      p.   cm.
  ISBN 0-89840-326-X
  1. Houck, Don. 2. Houck, LaDean. 3. Remarried people—United
States—Biography. 4. Remarriage—Religious aspects—Christianity.
I. Houck, LaDean. II. Title.
HG1019.U6H68   1991
306.84—dc20   91-4962
                                                        CIP

Unless indicated otherwise, Scripture quotations are from the *King James Version.*
  Scripture quotations designated NAS are from *The New American Standard Bible,* © The
Lockman Foundation 1960, 1962, 1963, 1968, 1971, 1972, 1975, 1977.
  Scripture quotations designated NIV are from *The Holy Bible: New International Version,*
© 1973, 1978, 1984 by the International Bible Society. Published by Zondervan Bible
Publishers, Grand Rapids, Michigan.
  Scripture quotations designated TLB are from *The Living Bible,* © 1971 by Tyndale
House Publishers, Wheaton, Illinois.

Cover design by Cornerstone Graphics
Cover photography by Visual Impact

For More Information, Write:
L.I.F.E.—P.O. Box A399, Sydney South 2000, Australia
Campus Crusade for Christ of Canada—Box 300, Vancouver, B.C., V6C 2X3, Canada
Campus Crusade for Christ—Pearl Assurance House, 4 Temple Row, Birmingham, B2 5HG, England
Lay Institute for Evangelism—P.O. Box 8786, Auckland 3, New Zealand
Campus Crusade for Christ—P.O. Box 240, Raffles City Post Office, Singapore 9117
Great Commission Movement of Nigeria—P.O. Box 500, Jos, Plateau State Nigeria, West Africa
Campus Crusade for Christ International—Arrowhead Springs, San Bernardino, CA 92414, U.S.A.

*We dedicate this book to our three sons,
David, Paul and Trey.*

*You have cried with us, laughed with us,
prayed with us, and are growing with us.
We've worked hard, but it's been a lot of fun.*

We love you guys!

Contents

Acknowledgments

We wish to thank the following people for allowing God to use them in a vital way to help us on our journey to harmony . . .

Dennis Baw, our first pastor, for spending hours with us before and after the wedding to help keep us together in the early years.

Brooke Annis, for counseling us "off our mountains" toward marital health, and for reading our manuscript for psychological soundness.

Florence Littauer, for being our mentor in growing our ministry, and for insisting we write our story to give hope and help to others. Thank you for being Paul to us.

Marita Littauer, for writing *Shades of Beauty* that introduced us to CLASS. You never cease to encourage and inspire us. Thank you for always believing in us.

Marilyn Heavilin, precious friend, for lovingly reading our chapters and teaching us how to say what we wanted to say.

David George, our pastor, for reading our manuscript for theological soundness and for not letting us off the hook until we clarified our principles. Thank you for believing what we teach is valuable for others to know.

Jean Bryant, our editor, for becoming a friend and catching a bit of our vision—Blended Blessings.

Barb Sherrill, our "other" editor, for understanding from the beginning what we were all about.

Dan Benson, of Here's Life Publishers, for believing

this book could happen, and lovingly encouraging us to complete the project.

Bart Bernstein, attorney, teacher and friend, for gently counseling us in writing the financial chapter and keeping us legally correct.

Our Advisory Council, for constantly praying for us. We would not be what God is constructing without you. We love you.

Our children, especially Trey, for giving up many hours of time with us to allow freedom to work on this project. You guys are the best blessings God has given us.

Our parents, Jim and Lorene, for always listening and encouraging even though you sometimes didn't know where we were headed. You are so very important to both of us. And the memory of Earl and Claudian is one of following dreams.

And a special thanks to all those who allowed us to use their stories to help others.

We dearly love you all, and thank God for you.

Foreword

In the past ten years, I have had the opportunity to meet Don and LaDean Houck and train them as speakers. As I became aware of their ability to communicate and their genuine love for people, I added them to our staff of CLASS (Christian Leaders, Authors & Speakers Services).

Don and LaDean minister effectively to those blended families who are in times of turmoil and distress. Their seminars are very popular, and I suspect this book will be as well. *Remarried With Children* tells their life story and offers practical answers to those in need.

If you are having any marriage or childraising problems, you will find encouragement in this book. If you are considering a new marriage where children are involved, reading this book first is essential.

Florence Littauer
Author and Speaker

1

Miracle in the Making

Don

I quickly pulled into the driveway and grabbed the packages from the seat beside me. Juggling them all in both arms, I finally managed to get out of the car. *Our first Christmas as husband and wife,* I sighed contentedly, shutting the door with my elbow. LaDean's bright face flashed in my mind, and I smiled.

Trey, LaDean's ten-year-old son, threw the front door open and shouted into the living room, "He's back with his decorations!" Then he helped me deposit my boxes on the floor.

I climbed the attic stairs to help LaDean and Trey move their decorations to the living room. My sons, David and Paul, carefully examined the bare Christmas tree with its long, needle-heavy branches and voiced their approval. Pine aroma sweetened the air.

What a great way to start our two-week old marriage! I thought with satisfaction. *The Christmas spirit will really make us a family.*

LaDean pulled a strand of lights from her box, and I stood up and insisted calmly, "Let me see those."

She slowly handed them to me.

David began untangling the pile of old strands laying near the tree. "Dad, I'll make sure these work."

LaDean watched over his shoulder, a frown gathering on her forehead.

I plugged in my string of lights and threaded them to the back of the tree, anchoring a red bulb to a low-hanging branch.

"Mom," Trey piped behind my elbow, "he's starting at the bottom."

LaDean scurried over. "We always start at the top," she informed me.

"No, no," I countered. "Everyone knows you start from the bottom and work up. Otherwise you waste half the strand before you begin."

"Well," she huffed, "Trey and I have done it the wrong' way for years. And we've had a beautiful tree every Christmas."

The tone in her voice made hackles rise on the back of my neck. "Good thing I'm here to show you how to do things right."

Her face reddened. "My way isn't as good as yours? This is my house. Why don't you just let me do things my way in my own place?"

Her sharp words set me off, and our argument flared.

David, Paul and Trey worked silently behind us, putting the lights on the tree. Their faces were glum.

Finally during a lull in the harsh words, Trey tapped LaDean on the shoulder. "Mom, can we start putting the rest of the decorations on?"

She looked at him oddly, then glanced at the tree. "I guess so," she sighed.

With the argument ended, we all quietly placed

bows and hung bulbs. Christmas music wafted strangely around us.

At last the tree looked picture perfect. I turned off the lamps so we could see the lighted tree in the dark. But even the twinkling lights and softly shining bulbs didn't erase the harsh words. Our Christmas joy had been shattered like a fragile ornament.

Building on Broken Pieces

When LaDean and I began our married lives, we were unprepared for the stress and problems involved in putting two families together. Soon after the ceremony, we ran headlong into many obstacles peculiar to families from previous broken relationships attempting to blend. Former traditions, habits and routines made compromise difficult. Complicated financial matters muddied our budget. Old hurts and feelings from earlier situations interfered with our new relationship. The presence of children with their own problems compounded the difficulties.

LaDean and I were shocked at the startling statistics about marriage in our culture: 50 percent of first marriages, 60 percent of second marriages and 80 percent of third marriages fail within five years.[1] We determined that, despite our own obstacles, we would not become one of those broken unions. Tragically, we were already on the road to divorce . . . again.

If you too are trying to build a relationship on the pieces of unhappy former marriages, you probably experience many of the same stresses and difficulties we encountered. Maybe you despair of ever achieving oneness out of such hurtful pasts. Thoughts of giving up and leaving run through your mind often.

We experienced these same feelings. We were both mired in the "I'm always right, don't confuse me with the facts" attitude and struggled with giving up "my" power for "we" power. For a long time, we muddled through our problems without any guidance.

Finally we began the rebuilding process by seeking help, first from our pastor, Dennis Baw, and then from our counselor, Brooke Annis, clinical director of Professional Service Associates, Inc. in Hurst, Texas. Our decision to ask for outside advice was tough to make. But as we put into practice what the counselors suggested, we began to develop effective principles for blending our lives. These became the foundation for the first conference we held, which we called "Blended Blessings."

As we gained experience in the dynamics of blended families through our own circumstances and those of others at the conferences, we saw that separation and divorce are almost never the answer—in fact, they create even greater problems. We also realized the deep need for a how-to book on blended living, a book that would help other couples avoid the cycle of divorce and that would help them rebuild their family unit.

The Process of Reconstruction

You may wonder if anyone can help you untangle the mess of emotions and hurts in your relationship. Through the years, we have found no simple answers to the complicated, painful problems that threaten blended marriages. But there are answers. Our God is a God of *hope*. He is a master at taking broken pieces and creating whole, beautiful relationships. He can help you enhance what you have, focus on the good qualities and habits you bring to your union, and make your marriage stronger.

I issue my strongest coach's pep talk to you husbands. Stay with this book and allow God, the builder of real men, to change you. Be willing to receive God's leading as He chooses to reveal it to you. Remember that, when we ask Him for a change in our lives, He doesn't send telegrams or letters—He sends people.

Tom Landry once said, "Coaching men is a process of making them do things they don't want to do in order for them to have what they really want." Marriage is a lot like that. There is great joy to be had. Please don't let your pride rob you of this joy.

Dr. C. R. Solomon, in his poem called "Heart to Heart," describes much better than we can the comfort in traveling with others who have experienced similar difficulties:

> When we come to the place of full retreat,
>   And our heart cries out for GOD,
> The only person whose heart ours can meet
>   Is the one who has likewise trod.
> Others may offer a word of cheer
>   To lift us from despair,
> But above the rest, the one we hear
>   Is the whisper, "I've been there."

So we urge you to join us in the difficult but fulfilling process of reconstructing your own marriage. Together we can battle old habits, conquer debilitating thoughts and feelings, and build new ways of relating to our partners.

Please don't think we have written this book to share a horror story of irreparable hurts. There is a happy ending!

The Journey Begins

Whether you are single again and reconsidering wedding vows, are struggling in a blended relationship, or have a strong marriage, we believe you'll find a set of principles you can use on your journey to what we call a "miracle marriage."

As we've learned and grown together, our experience has been like a long-distance drive in a car. Join us as we start on a road where you'll encounter detours, rough pavement, caution signs and construction zones.

You'll find there are times when you'll have to yield, and other times when you'll want to make a U turn, but you can't. And like any long car trip, you'll have times of smooth sailing and times when you want nothing more than to get out of the car!

But the drive is worth the effort when you've reached your final destination. We assure you, this journey has everlasting rewards.

2

Potholes and Deep Ruts

Don

Only the grace of God has kept LaDean and me from becoming a divorce statistic again. From the day we first met, our beginning as a couple resembled a trail filled with potholes and deep ruts. Caution signs were posted everywhere. Neither of us were completely aware of the hidden dangers we faced, but the threat of another failure got our attention, and we invited God to show us the weak areas in our lives and help us build a healthy relationship.

To help you understand the process we went through to blend our separate lives, we want to share our rocky beginnings. LaDean tells her story first.

LaDean

After the breakup of a difficult marriage that left me feeling devastated and defeated, I never wanted to remarry. I didn't trust anyone and decided not to let anyone get that close to me again. I couldn't handle another divorce and its failure.

My friends told me that a divorce was a new beginning. It was supposed to be exciting and fun. For me it was an ending, and depression was the only thing I felt.

After a while, I began dating again to have some adult conversation. Going out also provided a "free meal." Many times my date included Trey, and he got a free meal too. With my drastically reduced income, this was a welcome help to my food budget.

At first, dating was scary and uncomfortable. But the more I forced myself to get out of the house and start working on relationships with others, the easier I began to feel about dating. I even began to feel better about myself and was able to enjoy the friendships I was developing.

Sometimes, though, rather than working through any complications, I ended these relationships. I thought, *That is the nice part of being single. I can do just what I want.* I was becoming a "flaky single."

Finally, I began seeing one man more than the others. Although I didn't want to marry him, something continued to draw me to him. I even found myself turning down other dates just in case he wanted to be with me.

My feelings for this man scared me—we weren't compatible. Don was too religious, too demanding and too newly divorced. But he was also sensitive, masculine and very aware of me. I thought I had my life in order, but these feelings didn't fit into my plans. So I took a new approach.

"Don't you think you should date other women?" I suggested. "After all, you've been single such a short time." I told myself he needed time to heal and to figure out who he was before he got serious with another person. "It's all right with me," I assured him, "if you date someone else."

I soon realized that was a mistake. Every time I knew he was with someone else, my heart ached.

I felt as though I were losing control of my life. I didn't want these feelings—I didn't want to get close to anyone again. And I didn't want to marry Don! He just wasn't what I wanted.

So every time I found myself getting close to him, I pushed him away. Before long, this emotional yo-yo began messing up my head, and I decided I just wouldn't see him anymore.

I was determined, but it seemed that every time we tried to avoid each other, we somehow ended up back together. One Friday night Trey and I planned a quiet evening at home. I went to pull down the window shade, and I noticed a young man standing across the street. It was the same man who had burglarized my home several months before!

Instinctively, I yanked down the shade and grabbed for the phone. I knew my parents weren't home, and the only other number I could remember was Don's.

I dialed quickly. His masculine voice sounded so reassuring. I stammered into the receiver, "Don, that man is back. The one who broke into my house."

"Call your neighbor, and call the police. I'll be right there."

Little did I know he was in the middle of a romantic candlelight dinner. He immediately called a friend to take his date home and left for my house. Of course, that woman never went out with him again. It seemed as though God was working to bring us together.

So I began seeing him regularly, but our relationship was never smooth. After several months, for instance, Don announced he didn't think I was a Christian.

My mouth dropped open. "How can you even think that?" I was furious! "Just please take me home."

We didn't see each other for three weeks. During that time, I felt as though I were wandering in a wilderness, totally alone.

Through it all, my relationship with the Lord was beginning to change. I went from knowing *about* Him to *knowing* Him. I began to seek His will for my life. And as I did, it seemed everywhere I went, Don was there. I shared with Don my experience of committing my life to the Lord, and that became a bonding force in our relationship and drew us even closer together.

The Marathon

One day, I found myself standing beside Don at the counter of the marriage license bureau. I couldn't believe it! Did I really want to take this step again?

After examining Don's papers, the clerk handed back one of his medical forms. "This has not been signed by your doctor."

He stared at the bottom line. A sheepish grin spread over his face. "Well, you can see I had my physical. Can't you take it anyway?"

The clerk shook her head. "I'm sorry."

My throat tightened. I couldn't believe this man was so inconsiderate of my time. How could he be so careless as to not even notice his papers were not in order for such an important occasion?

Don sighed and began folding up his documents. "Well, we'll just have to come back."

I couldn't believe my ears—and I shouted, "We *can't* come back! This is the only day I can come. I can't believe you didn't take care of this."

Everyone in the room looked at him, then at me, disbelief written all over their faces.

The clerk suggested I sign the license anyway. I hesitated. *Am I making a big mistake? If Don can't take care of this simple matter, how can he take care of me?* But I pushed aside my misgivings and grabbed a pen and the license.

All my legal names barely fit on the line. Don peered over my shoulder. "Well, I guess this will be the last time you can get married," he chuckled loudly. "There's no room on that line for any more names!"

I glared at him.

This incident was the first serious indication of the rough road ahead. We were in "training" for a marathon—a marathon argument.

Premarital Jitters

On Friday evening, the week before our wedding, another "Caution—Rough Road Ahead" appeared. Don and I began discussing children, money, houses—and who remembers what else—in my living room. The "discussion" soon became a shouting match. At 2 A.M., Don announced hotly, "This wedding is off. Call all your friends and tell them not to come." And he stomped out.

I was crushed. Tears filled my eyes. How could I ever tell my friends?

I finally fell asleep, but at ten o'clock the next morning the doorbell rang. Don was standing on my front step when I opened the door.

My eyes narrowed to slits. "What do you want now? Haven't we argued enough?"

"I don't want to argue anymore. But can we talk?"

This man is driving me crazy, I thought. But I let him in.

Our discussion quickly turned into another marathon, both of us so intent on winning that neither of us could see what was going on inside the other. We fought sporadically through lunch and on into the afternoon.

By 5 P.M. things had deteriorated completely. "You are so hard-headed, I can't talk to you," Don seethed as he left in a huff, slamming the door behind him.

This time the wedding really was called off. I phoned my friend Sandy, and she consoled me for an hour. By the time I put the receiver down, I was convinced the situation was not my fault. *Things happen for the best,* I decided. *It's better to find out how he is now than to discover it after we're married.* With that, I tried to dismiss the last few hours from my mind.

The next morning, Don phoned just before I left for church. His message was short: "I'll be in Pastor Baw's office at 10:30. If you want to be there, fine." And he hung up.

I stared at the phone. *Who does he think he is, telling me what to do? You can just visit with Dennis yourself, buster!*

Then a little voice inside me said, *You could be blowing your whole future.*

Well, maybe so. I could go to Dennis' office and just listen. (That would be different.) I wouldn't have to commit to anything if I didn't say anything. I shrugged. *I'll go.*

When I arrived, Dennis and Don were making small talk, waiting for me. (I hadn't fooled anyone.)

After I took my chair, Dennis asked, "Well, what's the problem?"

I waited for Don to answer. (Remember, I had decided just to listen.)

"For starters," Don began, "LaDean and her ex-husband had a cabinet full of liquor in the utility room. I told her she should dispose of it, but she refused. That's going to be my home. If she really loved me, she would do what I asked."

I couldn't believe what I was hearing. Of all the things we had "discussed," why had Don chosen to discuss the alcohol with a Baptist minister?

Dennis turned toward me. "How do you feel about this, LaDean?"

"I will remove the alcohol when I feel the need to. Not when someone else demands I get rid of it."

"I agree," Dennis nodded. "Don needs to let the Lord deal with you about the alcohol."

I smiled smugly, liking Dennis' assessment of the situation.

Then Dennis went on, "What does the alcohol represent to you, LaDean? Why don't you make this a matter of prayer?"

We discussed some of the other hot points in our relationship without coming to any conclusions. Then Dennis suggested, "Why don't the two of you go to lunch? I think you have a big case of premarital jitters."

That seemed like a good suggestion, so Don and I picked Trey up from his Sunday school class and drove to a quiet restaurant.

"You and I always seem to be talking over food," Don laughed as our waitress set down the orders. "Maybe food is the only thing we have in common."

I smiled coolly.

"I think Trey has had all the 'fun' he can handle," Don said ruefully.

I nodded. Trey must be ready for some "smooth pavement." So was I. Trey looked hopeful.

By the time we had finished our meal, we decided the wedding was on again.

The following week was filled with excitement. While preparing for the rehearsal, I felt no one could be as happy as I was. Last weekend's argument had been forgotten—well, maybe not completely forgotten, but pushed aside.

As we were practicing the ceremony, I decided not to use a stand-in; I wanted to walk through my part. The wedding party paraded to the altar. Then strangely, while rehearsing the vows, I burst into tears. Perhaps I was "in mourning"—I had worn a black dress. Black, like you wear to a funeral, not to a wedding celebration.

Concerned, Don's older son, David, caught my eye. "What should I do if you start crying during the ceremony tomorrow?"

"Don't be nice to me. Just ignore me."

What excellent advice from a soon-to-be stepmom to her stepson! And what a strange way for a happy bride-to-be to act. But I didn't want sympathy or attention. I wanted composure. And I wasn't sure I could maintain that if David were sympathetic.

Wedding Day

On our wedding day, I was awakened by the telephone. Don was on the line. "The men's fellowship at church met early this morning to pray for us on this special day. Do you know how important you are to me?" He went on to share some special thoughts about our relationship.

Suddenly, I felt he was the neatest, most sensitive man I had ever known. How fortunate I was to be marrying him! That conversation will always be a precious memory to me.

The rest of my morning was filled with errands, packing and excitement. Don had insisted on an afternoon wedding, and I thought all weddings should be at dusk. We had "compromised" and set the ceremony at 2 P.M. Now I was glad we had agreed on the earlier time.

I wore a gorgeous, full-length, cream-colored dress with antique lace and a delicate, antique-looking hat with a long veil that exactly matched the lace on the gown. (I am so glad I decided on that one rather than the red one I had originally selected.) I remember feeling beautiful.

Standing at the back of the church, waiting to walk down the aisle, I again had second thoughts. *I believe I could handle getting married if I just didn't have to walk down this aisle. But it's a little too late to run.*

My father tugged on my arm, and we moved into the sanctuary. The next thing I remember, I was on Don's arm, tripping over my dress as we climbed the steps to the altar. My legs shook, and I gripped his arm tighter.

We exchanged vows, and Pastor Dennis began to sing the Pat Terry song, "That's the Way." Don and I sang along with him as a commitment to each other. (This song and commitment time have been so special to us that we use them in our Blended Blessings conferences.) Everything about the wedding seemed rosy and wonderful.

Our reception was also marvelous. Trey played his guitar and sang. We visited with our special friends, laughed, cried and ate, and as we left, Paul showered us with birdseed. We looked so happy when the photographer snapped his last pictures.

Then the honeymoon began.

First we went to eat at the Mexican restaurant where we had gone on our first date. We were anticipating a romantic dinner for two with a lot of attention because we hadn't changed out of our wedding attire. We were shocked when my entire family—aunts, cousins, nieces, nephews and all—greeted us! We had a delightful evening but certainly not a romantic or intimate one.

Our wedding night was spent in my home. On Sunday, Don, who was a football coach, talked me into going to my parents' house to watch a game on TV. Somehow, the honeymoon was not progressing like I thought it should. Hadn't Don planned to whisk me away to a romantic condo in Colorado? But here we were, still in Arlington, Texas. Disappointed, I took a nap on the sofa.

As soon as the football game ended, I awoke. "You sure are some sensitive husband," I snipped.

He mouthed something back about my hard head, then said a little more brightly, "Let's go home and pack."

Is This a Honeymoon?

Finally, at ten o'clock on Sunday evening, we began our honeymoon trip. We had driven for an hour and a half when Don said he was too sick to go on. He pulled the car in at a motel in Wichita Falls.

I certainly wasn't prepared for what happened next. He made a beeline for the bathroom to get ready for bed. In minutes, he emerged in his white underwear and an ugly grey T-shirt with "Teesher, Teashear, Teecher, Teacher" down the front in bright blue letters. He fell onto the bed reeking of Vicks VapoRub and complaining about a light head from the Nyquil he had taken earlier.

You mean I married this? I cried silently.

Excusing myself, I went into the bathroom and looked in the mirror. "Okay, Lord," I whispered, "I have really blown it this time. This man you've sent me? I'm sending him back!"

After a few minutes, I pulled myself together and made my entrance into the bedroom in my new, delicate pink lace negligee. Don was sound asleep.

I cried myself to sleep.

We both felt better in the morning and headed for Amarillo. As we drove, I selected just the right time to delicately suggest, "Why don't you buy a nice pair of pajamas for our trip?" He reluctantly agreed.

We stopped at a shopping mall in Amarillo. When we left the car, I thought it odd that he turned toward Montgomery Wards and I started toward Colberts, an exclusive department store. But I took his hand submissively and went with him to Wards. Without a word, he quickly selected a horrible, brown, old-man-looking pair of pajamas.

Walking back to the car, I began to cry silently. *Why didn't he love me enough to bring some neat pajamas?* I wanted to throw up.

The closer we got to the car, the angrier I became. *How dare he do this to me? Why did we get married anyway? I should have stayed single.*

I have thought this many times since that first time,

but I have come to realize that, yes, my life was simpler before Don, but it was so thin.

I tried to approach the subject of these horrible pajamas very gently, but I just didn't know any easy way. "Don, couldn't you take those back and get something more acceptable?"

He was furious! He wheeled and strode toward the store, trying to walk ahead of me, and I ran behind, trying to keep up with him.

We went to Colberts and found some soft peach men's pajamas with white piping—on sale. I was so pleased.

Don stalked back to the car, unlocked the doors, and got in behind the wheel without saying a word. He started the motor, jammed the car into reverse and tromped on the gas—and we shot out of the parking space right into the car behind us.

When he jumped out to see what the damage was, I leaned back, my nerves taut, my heart heavy. *This is a nightmare—not a honeymoon! Will my life always be this difficult?*

Fortunately, the cars hadn't been damaged. We left the parking lot and continued silently on our way. About two blocks later, I announced, "This is not working out. Just take me home."

Don replied stiffly, "I'll be glad to." He turned the car around and headed back to Arlington.

I couldn't believe he was doing this. Our marriage was going to end in divorce, and we hadn't even had a honeymoon. Didn't he love me? I felt panicky.

After we had traveled a couple of miles, I suggested meekly, "Since we already paid for the condo, maybe we should go ahead and use it."

"Guess we would lose our investment." He turned the car around again and silently drove on.

This was exhausting. I decided to take a nap. (I

always eat or sleep in times of crisis.) By the time we arrived in Raton, New Mexico, I was sick, physically sick—of Don and of this relationship.

In the motel, Don medicated himself, pulled on his new pajamas and fell asleep.

I slipped into the bathroom. Looking in the mirror and thinking I had really botched it this time, I prayed. "I am trying to trust You, Lord, but this is so hard. Don is not at all what I thought he would be. Oh, Lord, don't let me down now, and please don't leave me. I can't do this on my own." A sweet comfort filled my heart.

The Ski Trip

We finally made it to Winter Park, Colorado. Now maybe our honeymoon could begin. I was ready for fun, romance and some exciting skiing.

But we were both so out of shape that the skiing sapped what little energy we had left. Each evening, we would eat a bite and crash. Our honeymoon became a ritual of swallowing Nyquil, applying Vicks to our chests, and saying, "Goodnight. I'll see you in the morning."

We did have our fun moments. I have fond memories of crawling up the stairs at night because our bodies ached and because we were laughing so hard we couldn't stand up.

I loved the snowball fights, the long walks, the moonlight hayride and the intimate dinners we shared. I tucked them away in the closets of my heart. And what fun we had in our tiny condo cooking together in the kitchen!

With a beginning like this, though, it's a miracle we survived. Only the grace of God could help us. The longer Don and I are married, the more convinced I am we are part of God's plan.

When you read Don's version of our courtship, wedding and honeymoon, you will realize how little we understood or knew about each other. Looking back makes me realize how much God has taught me to soften, salvage and savor.

```
┌─────────────────────────────┐
│     CAUTION—TRUCK           │
│       ENTRANCE              │
└─────────────────────────────┘
```

3

Mr. Perfect

Don

O, God, here I am a statistic, a divorce statistic! It had been so painful I could hardly say the word. Instead, I told people, "I'm not married right now."

I had never learned how to deal with failure. I was raised on the Lone Ranger, Tonto and Roy Rogers—all those guys who could always make things come out right. Why couldn't I do the same? How had "Mr. Perfect" messed up so horribly?

I still recall the helplessness I felt. I had disappointed the whole world, and especially my mother. My divorce was the crowning blow in a long line of failures that I had inflicted on her. How could I face her?

After all, my mother had raised me to be a hero. She and my great-grandmother, who was dear to me, had always called me their "special" boy. Whenever things went wrong, I was made to feel I could make everything right. I tried my best to live up to the role they put me in. But the harder I worked, the more I failed.

My first big predicament came in 1959. As a college student, I learned that a girl I had dated in high school was pregnant. The child was mine so I married the girl to "fix" the situation. I then dishonored her and myself by abandoning and divorcing her after the baby was born.

My second marriage was to my college sweetheart in 1960. In 1969 my wife and I divorced and then we remarried, and I planned to start all over again. But within ten years, in 1979, we finalized our second divorce. My two teenage sons lived with me, but they didn't know what to do with this dad who couldn't get himself together. My self-image went west on a load of pipe dreams. For years I had been a Sunday school teacher and a faithful church attender and a husband. Now, how could God ever use me again?

Withdrawing behind a wall of self-pity, I tuned the world completely out and grew into a real, live couch potato. For hours I sat and thought about my failed marriage. Surely, there was some outside reason why it hadn't worked for me. Someone "out there" had to be blamed for my failures. Why else would a gentle, easygoing, God-fearing man like me be rocking in the wake of a failed marriage and a shattered ego?

My situation was so grim that my brother, a law officer, stopped by the house nearly every night. It wasn't until years later that he told me how worried he was about my mental and emotional condition.

Finally, I decided marriage just wasn't for me. Surely I could find a way to live without so much pain. An intimate relationship involved too much risk, and women were too fickle. They didn't know what they wanted. The only way I could stay single and sane was to put the responsibility for my failure on someone else. I convinced myself that my ex-wife was wrong and that I was right.

My friends encouraged me to think that way. After all, I was the one doing the right things—raising the boys, going to church, supporting the family.

In resolving my conflict by blaming others, I made

everyone around me acknowledge Don the Perfect. Eventually, my attitude caused my friends to pull away, too. It was several years before I learned that my choleric, strong-willed, bulldozer personality, which was effective in coaching football, stunk when it came to other people—especially when it came to marriage.

About that same time, my career fell apart. I lost my coaching position. Since being fired is a coaching hazard, I knew it could happen to anyone—except, of course, to Don, Mr. Perfect.

Even though I was divorced, I still attended the couples' class at church for a time because I could not turn loose my desire to be part of a couple. Eventually though, I felt uncomfortable in the group, so I quit going for a while. Finally I broke down and visited the singles class.

The singles accepted me as I was. I could play the "poor little me" game, and my new friends would support me. So I climbed back up on my mountain of perfection, built my defenses and played Mr. Wonderful.

The Storm Begins

Then someone entered my bubble. *This frightened-acting, vulnerable woman,* I thought, *looks like a good candidate to adore me. She is beautiful and sensitive. Surely she will appreciate my perfection.*

Though I was physically attracted to her, I was suspicious at the same time and outspoken about my distrust. I did not reveal much of myself to her, especially not my weaknesses or failures. So our courtship was stormy. We didn't have disagreements or even arguments—we had *fights.*

Because I had never learned to fight fair, I tried to make LaDean look as wrong as possible. This was easy for me since I already had forty years experience at blaming others.

Many times I accused her, "All I am doing is trying

to be right. I'm not hurting anyone. Why do you want to do all these bad things to me?"

Or I played the role of bulldozer. "I have done so many good things for you. You see how wonderful I treat you. Why is it you will not do things my way?" My ex-wife remarkably had endured this treatment for years.

In spite of all that, LaDean and I had some good experiences during the year we dated. We had a chemistry that drew us together, and gradually, both of us came to believe we were destined to marry. So whenever our relationship hit another stormy period, I would pray, "Please, God, take control of this."

Finally, we set a wedding date, but trying to get married was a bucket of worms in itself. I made an appointment with LaDean to take her to the marriage license bureau. How excited I was to escort her to the counter!

The clerk was efficient. She examined LaDean's papers, then reached for mine. Smiling broadly, I confidently handed them across the counter.

The clerk took a second look at the form from my doctor. "This has not been signed by your doctor," she said as she slid it back to me.

I looked over the paper. It seemed like such an unimportant item. I had passed the exam, everything was in order—except for that one line at the bottom.

"Well, you can see I had my physical. Can't you take it anyway?" I smiled.

The clerk pursed her lips firmly. "I'm sorry."

I turned to LaDean. "Well, we'll just have to come back later."

Her face resembled a gathering storm cloud. "We can't come back! This is the only day I can come. I can't believe you didn't take care of this."

Feeling panicky, I looked around. Everyone in the room was staring at us. *They probably think I mismanaged the whole affair, instead of messing up some lousy unimportant paper.* I snapped back, "It's no big deal. Why do you make such a scene over such a small thing?"

The clerk suggested to LaDean, "Why don't you sign the license anyway?"

LaDean grabbed the pen and began filling in the blank. I tried to diffuse her anger with a joke about all her names fitting on the line, but she began fuming about my lack of responsibility.

That made me angrier. No self-respecting Mr. Perfect would fail in that area, would he?

Soon we were staging one of our marathon arguments right there at the counter. I wish now that I could have known what the clerk was thinking while all this was going on. We must have been a hoot! By the time we left the building, neither one of us was speaking.

We continued our war the rest of the week.

"You just can't get your act together!" LaDean accused.

"Well, you expect too much!" I'd retort.

"If you loved me, you'd see that things were done right."

"If you loved me, you wouldn't try to tell me what to do."

By Saturday, a week before the wedding, I had had enough. "This wedding is off. Call all your friends and tell them not to come." Without another word, I stormed out of the house.

Birdseed and Well-wishes

I really don't know why I reconsidered my decision, but I sensed forces working in this situation that were beyond my control. So the next morning, I called our pastor, Dennis Baw. "Would you have time to meet with me right away?"

"Well . . . my schedule is pretty tight." He paused. "How about during the Sunday school hour?"

"Fine, I'll be there."

I called LaDean to inform her of the meeting. *She can come if she wants,* I thought as I dialed her number, *but I hope she doesn't show. She may say something that will make me look wrong.* When she answered, I announced, "I'll be in Pastor Baw's office at 10:30. If you want to be there, fine." Then I hung up.

Of course she came.

The first thing Dennis asked was, "Well, what's the problem?"

LaDean didn't answer. To cover my uneasiness, I brought up LaDean's liquor cabinet. That would show the pastor how wrong she was.

But Dennis didn't jump right on her. Instead, he turned to her. "How do you feel about this, LaDean?"

Quickly, the conversation changed to make me look like the one in the wrong. Dennis even suggested that I let God deal with LaDean about this issue. How could God do that without my help?

I finally gave in about the alcohol (I knew Dennis was right), and I realized I loved LaDean and did want to marry her. Even before we left the office, I committed myself to go ahead with the wedding.

During lunch, LaDean and I discussed some of the areas in which we disagreed. The entire time, I was thinking, *Why does everything have to be a power struggle? If she would only accept my leadership and not fight me, we could be a lot happier.*

Our wedding day was wonderful. The weather turned beautiful, and all our good friends came.

But when I walked out behind the groomsmen at the front of the church, I suddenly got a terrible case of wedding jitters. My knees began to buckle. Mr. Perfect was so unnerved that he almost passed out in front of all his friends and relatives!

As I turned to my son David standing beside me, intending to ask him to help hold me up, I saw LaDean waiting at the back of the sanctuary. She was gorgeous in her beautiful wedding dress. I couldn't back out now.

She moved down the aisle on her father's arm, and a new strength took hold of me. I slipped my hand under her arm and helped her up the steps to the altar.

As the pastor sang a commitment song and played the guitar, LaDean and I sang along. A sense of peace flowed through me as I promised to honor her until death. Little did I know that God would take me at my word and ask me to work through the tough times ahead. But at the moment, the task of husband and father seemed an easy road.

Our reception was fun. I enjoyed every moment. We left in a blizzard of birdseed and well-wishes. Now for the honeymoon! Lots of fun, right? But how can a honeymoon be "honey" when it is controlled by killer bees?

I had planned to take LaDean, dressed in her lovely gown, to the first restaurant I had taken her to. When we arrived, there was her entire family, already seated. Our romantic time together became a family gathering, full of laughter and fun. We had a good time. Right from the start, LaDean's family accepted me as a son.

Then I took LaDean to her house for our first night together. The next morning, I remembered the football game on television. "LaDean," I suggested enthusiastically, "let's watch the game with your parents this afternoon."

Her face clouded over. I figured she would get over her irritation in a few moments.

But she didn't. At her parents' house, she promptly settled into the sofa and took a nap. Despite her obvious displeasure, I enjoyed the game with the rest of the family. Then we left on our honeymoon. Now the real fun could begin! (Enter the killer bees!)

"Take Me Home"

As we neared Wichita Falls, I began to feel sick. My head was reeling and my stomach churning. I found the first available motel room, downed some cold medicine, put Vicks on my chest and slid into my comfortable "Teesher, Teashear, Teecher, Teacher" T-shirt.

That T-shirt caused a mild thunderstorm. LaDean stared at it aghast, and then fled to the bathroom.

How can she love me and not accept me as I am? I thought, shocked. But I was too sick to care. So I dropped myself into the bed and fell asleep immediately.

On the way to Amarillo the next day, LaDean suggested, "Why don't you buy a nice pair of pajamas for our trip?"

To give in to this hard-headed person, I stopped at Montgomery Wards and bought a pair.

"Don, couldn't you take these back and get something more acceptable?" she said when we got nearly back to the car.

Why on earth didn't she buy them herself if she's so picky? I grabbed the package, and we stomped back into the mall. By the time we exchanged the pajamas and left the store, I was so mad I could only think I had made the biggest mistake of my life.

Reaching the car, I opened LaDean's door and tossed the package into the back. Coming around, I slid into the driver's seat and slammed the door. LaDean stared out the passenger window.

I started the engine, slammed the car into reverse, shoved on the gas—and backed out of the parking place into another car. Horrified, I jumped out of the car to see what I'd done. To my relief, I had only hit another car's bumper. No damage!

I pulled out of the parking lot, slowly now, and we headed for the freeway. LaDean's voice seemed cold and indifferent as she broke the silence. "Just take me home. This isn't working out."

"I'll be glad to," I agreed. This was the pits. And we turned around.

After a few miles, LaDean said, "Since the condo is already paid for, I guess we could go ahead and stay there."

This is crazy! I thought. But I said, "Guess we should not lose our investment." So I turned the car back toward Colorado. As we drove, my thoughts formed a prayer. *God, I don't want to talk to her. Please put her to sleep.* Soon she dozed off, and I exhaled in long, slow relief.

Our skiing honeymoon in Winter Park went better. I love the mountains and found that LaDean does, too. But she also got sick, and on many of our nights she smelled of Vicks, wore her full-length granny gown, and said to me, "Goodnight. See you in the morning." This was marital bliss?

Despite the problems, we found a fulfilling physical relationship. We developed a bond that was to hold us together during tough times later.

I had stretched the honeymoon budget so tightly that we used our last five dollars at the Dairy Queen in Decatur, Texas, forty miles from home. We treated ourselves to a cheeseburger and fries, which we shared, and two drinks. We pulled into the driveway of our new home—not badly bent, but literally broke. My financial irresponsibility was to be a source of future conflict.

As chaotic and stressful as our honeymoon was, there were some dynamics working there that would actually be good for us in the years to come. One especially important factor was our willingness to stay with our relationship. If either of us really had wanted out of the marriage, that person had plenty of opportunities. But neither LaDean nor I would give up.

The principles my family had taught me served us well during those early days. My parents had stressed seeing things through. The grass may look greener somewhere else, but it is still grass, and it must be mowed fertilized, watered, trimmed and cared for just like any other grass. Life is a process, not a series of one-time happenings which can't be rectified. I'm grateful for my parents' counsel.

But it took me thirty years and a fourth marriage to realize that I could royally mess up my life and still survive to be used by God again. Although I began to admit that I brought problems from my former marriage into my new one, I was not yet willing to take responsibility for my actions and feelings. I believe this gap between knowing something in our head and making it happen and work in the way we live is a major cause of stress in our world and of many marriage breakups.

If you recognize your situation somewhere in our story, have *hope*. Please don't expect this book to help you decide to get a divorce and find someone else who will be perfect for you. You will never meet such a partner. But with the proper help, you can learn to deal with your most difficult marital problems. You will discover, as we have, that many of the weaknesses in your relationship can be changed into strengths.

We will begin with simple steps to set your direction. Then we will move into more difficult phases of marriage-building to encourage and enrich your journey. LaDean will begin with the first step—to affirm your commitment for the difficult task ahead.

4

The Big "C" Word

LaDean

Do you remember being single? You could easily end a dating relationship when it began to require more from you than you were willing to give. You never had to step too far out of your comfort zone into an unknown closeness. And you could keep emotional risks to a minimum.

But the day you repeated your wedding vows, things changed. Suddenly your mate began making demands on you. So did his or her family. No longer could you draw back into your safe shell like a wise old turtle when the storms began to rage. Instead, you found the tempest was really brewing inside your protected place.

We experienced this dilemma.

One evening, Don and I were in the kitchen arguing in loud voices. In fact, we were screaming about something neither of us can remember now. It was one of the worst fights since our wedding day.

Finally, Don doubled up his fist, pounded on the

cabinet, rattling dishes in the cupboard, and yelled at me, "I am not leaving! I don't care what you do!"

My mouth dropped open. I was stunned! Until this moment, I thought leaving was an option for both of us. Many times, I feared Don would walk out on me. Now he was telling me he wouldn't bail out no matter what happened.

Suddenly, I realized we could start from this moment and approach our relationship on a higher level of commitment than we ever had before. Relief poured over me. "You're not leaving," I asked with deep emotion, "no matter what I do?"

"No ma'am! I am not!" he answered with a determined look in his eyes.

That moment was a turning point in our marriage.

No matter what shape your marriage is in, you can begin right where you are to establish a new relationship. As husband and wife, you can be all that God wants you to be. He will give you the strength to go on. But that takes a decision to go ahead despite the costs.

The Foundation of Marriage

While traveling and speaking in many parts of the country, we have observed that both Christian and non-Christian viewpoints on marriage have one similarity. They see the big "C" word, Commitment, as the number-one reason marriages stay intact. Indeed, every human being desires the rewards and security that lie in the dedication two people have for each other.

We all understand the importance of totally giving oneself to another person, of listening and sharing in the nitty-gritty details of everyday life, and of making life's major decisions together. Then why are so many people afraid to make commitments? The fear of change has a lot to do with this. We may be afraid that if we allow ourselves to change, the new us will not be accepted. Or that the person with whom we share our innermost feelings will not share with us. And for those of us who have experienced the failure of a relationship in the past, we certainly recall the pain of commitments that have been broken.

Despite the risk, the big "C" word is still the foundation for marriage. Commitment is sharing the joys of intertwining your life with another. It does not mean the loss of individuality; it means having the confidence to trust in closeness even when you are apart. It is deciding that you will never make a U turn to go back to the days before you accepted the responsibility of this marriage.

Commitment is an action word. It becomes a force in your life, and it requires a great deal from you. Yet when you follow through on your promise, you can lead your family in freedom and victory.

Jan, for example, felt like giving up when her second husband, Luke, quit a well-paying job for another one making much less money. Within a couple of months, they began having financial difficulties. Luke had a daughter from a previous marriage, and he paid monthly child support payments to his ex-wife. That stretched Jan's household budget to the limit. She resented paying Luke's ex-wife when her own family suffered.

Sometimes, Jan wondered if she could take the pressure. She found it hard to vent her frustration, though, since she realized Luke had an obligation as a father to his daughter. But the situation still didn't seem fair.

Soon, Luke and Jan were several thousand dollars in debt. Jan continued to make every dollar count, and in time, Luke found a better position and they were able to slowly put their finances back in order. Their relationship became stronger because of Jan's willingness to stick with Luke through their financial hardship.

We admit that being committed to each other is not easy but we do not fight the battle alone. Our God fights for us (Deuteronomy 20:4). He will equip us with everything we need to build a wholesome, godly relationship (Hebrews 13:20,21).

We encourage you to begin your journey with a covenant between yourself and the Lord.

The Covenant

When you accepted Jesus Christ as your personal Savior, you made a choice to enter God's family. If you have never asked Jesus Christ to be your Savior, we encourage you to read Appendix A to discover the love and forgiveness He offers you. The decision you make to follow Him will be the most important step of your life.

In turn, He promised to never leave you nor forsake you (Hebrews 13:5). And He will give you the power and strength to build a marital partnership for life. But God also asks something of you: Surrender every part of yourself to His control. That's your covenant with God. The apostle Paul writes:

> I urge you therefore, brethren, by the mercies of God, to present your bodies a living and holy sacrifice, acceptable to God, which is your spiritual service of worship. And do not be conformed to this world, but be transformed by the renewing of your mind, that you may prove what the will of God is, that which is good and acceptable and perfect (Romans 12:1,2, NAS).

You and your spouse need to make a covenant between the two of you as well. Let us share a covenant we have used in our conferences. Prayerfully and honestly fill in the blanks, then date and sign it, asking the Lord for the strength and faithfulness to keep your commitment to Him. File the covenant where you can find it when you need encouragement. During times of growth and success, use it to remind yourself of how far you have come. Let this covenant be a memento of the "miracle marriage" the Lord is helping you construct.

My Covenant

Dearest Lord Jesus,

You have directed me to *Remarried With Children* because You knew I had needs in my life. You are causing me to examine my heart and realize I must work prayerfully to overcome the following weaknesses:

_____

_____

You are causing me to become aware of the following strengths that You can use in rebuilding this relationship:

_____

_____

You are showing me this is a new beginning. You have given me another chance to blend my life with someone else's life. I set the following goals and priorities to give You the freedom to accomplish this in me:

_____

_____

I know that in order to receive the blessings You have for me I must commit to You:

_____

_____

Beginning today, I will allow Your holy love to flow through me to _____.

Signature _____ Date _____

(Permission is given to the reader to photocopy this Covenant for personal use.)

Miracle Marriage

The longer we are married, the more strongly we believe we have experienced a miracle. Our journey has been filled with struggles, yet the power of God's grace and forgiveness has strengthened our relationship beyond our expectations.

As you travel down a similar road, claim God's blessings on your marriage, too. The apostle Peter advises:

> To sum up, let all be harmonious, sympathetic, brotherly, kindhearted, and humble in spirit; not returning evil for evil, or insult for insult, but giving a blessing instead; for you were called for the very purpose that you might inherit a blessing (1 Peter 3:8,9, NAS).

Reacting in a loving, godly way to disagreements, tensions and hurts will heap blessings on your relationship. And it will bring healing to old wounds.

As you commit yourselves to the Lord and to a new beginning in your marriage, we are sure you, too, will discover a miracle in your lives, and that you will be well on your way to a lifelong bond.

5

The Common Thread— Bonding

Don

Imagine you're driving down a highway during rush-hour traffic. Above your lane, a huge yellow sign reads, "Left lane ends." Ahead you notice traffic merging from two lanes into one.

Turning on your blinker, you check the rear view mirror to gauge the traffic flow. A space opens in front of a red van. The driver brakes slightly to give you room so you skillfully slip into place.

Bonding in a blended marriage resembles these merging lanes. A man and woman join separate lifestyles and personalities into one unit. Although the relationship allows for diversity and individuality, the couple places their commitment to each other above all else in decisions and actions.

The Bible describes this bonding process: "For this cause a man shall leave his father and his mother and shall cleave to his wife; and they shall become one flesh" (Genesis 2:24, NAS).

Such joining produces unity and agreement. Bonding, so essential to marital stability and harmony, is the common thread throughout this book.

Many couples act like they have and appear to be bonded, but when we see that they lack commitment to their relationship, we know they have not truly bonded. Generally, neither have couples who never disagree. In truth, silence may not always be golden; sometimes it is yellow. Frequently, husbands and wives in second and third marriages simply refuse to confront issues with their mates because of past experiences.

One area that poses danger to bonding is the transition from dating to marriage. We learn a lot about romancing and getting to the altar, but not much about what a couple is. Dating couples nurture and care for their relationship as a precious treasure, but then they cross the wedding threshold and the emphasis immediately shifts to position rather than intimacy. The dashing young Casanova gets caught up in being "husband" and begins to view his mate as "wife" more than confidante and lover. And his wife begins to treat him in the same way.

Soon both are entangled in *what* they are and lose perspective of *who* they are, and their relationship suffers. The good news, though, is that the couple can correct the situation and experience bonding, sometimes on their own—if not, there is help available.

A blended family compounds the problems. Many couples bring pain, anger and fear into a second marriage. Blended families have learned that husbands and wives come and go. Whether through death or divorce, these people have experienced the non-permanent mate, so commitments are harder to make.

To build a bonded relationship, a couple must overcome a number of obstacles: power struggles, tunnel vision, selfishness, territorial rights, having-things-my-way attitudes, role stereotypes, anger and bitterness, fairy-tale mentality, and many more. These barriers inhibit or prevent bonding by causing separations in spirit between a husband and wife.

Is bonding impossible in a blended marriage? LaDean and I have seen many discouraged couples grow in unity after they had almost given up. But the effort to become one flesh will test the strength of your commitment to each other.

When the Pieces Won't Fit

Bonding in a blended family is like trying to put a huge jigsaw puzzle together. Do you remember your frustrations as a child when you tried to get one piece into place? You worked and worked, and you turned the piece every which way, but it wouldn't fit. Maybe you wanted to grab a pair of scissors and trim the piece to make it slip into place—never mind that the whole puzzle would be mismatched.

Sometimes a blended family will try to trim the pieces of their relationships like that to make them fit. It looks like the puzzle is coming together right, but then several pieces don't match anywhere—and the challenge intensifies.

In working with couples, we have discovered common puzzle pieces that are difficult to fit in. We call these "dynamics to blend." We would like to identify a few of these found in most blended marriages. LaDean begins by describing the dangers of diminished coupling.

LaDean
_____

1. Diminished Coupling

A couple marrying for the first time usually has at least nine months to enjoy being "just the two of them."

They have time to visit casually, observe each other at leisure, and contemplate and plan where they are going without the stress of children. Blended couples have no such luxury.

Newlyweds in a first marriage need time and space together, but when you marry again you pick up where everyone's life left off. We have found that most blended partners fail to recognize they know no more about each other than newlyweds. The pressures of a family take away from the carefree joy of discovering new things about each other. They have no time to grow together before children appear. There is no time for intimacy to happen spontaneously. It must be planned like everything else.

As a woman, I faced some particular tensions—like changing my name again. I had an established career. Everyone knew me by my former married name, and I resented constantly explaining my marital status.

As a single in 1979, I had trouble doing some of the things a married person takes for granted. My application for a credit card was denied. I was furious and I felt rejected. When I eventually did develop a credit rating under my own name, I did not want to give it up for any man. I thought, *Suppose this marriage doesn't work?* So, preparing for the worst, I retained my name and my credit rating. Still, I must say it was during this time that I began to be willing to trust Don's and my relationship.

Another consideration was Trey. We had shared the same last name. I thought, *If I change my name, the world will know we're a split family. That'll embarrass both of us.*

These pressures prevented me from breaking ties with my previous life and bonding with my new one. Harmony was not growing very fast.

Several other factors, however, did help to unify our relationship. One was the kindness and love Don showed for Trey. One of my unspoken requirements for marriage was that my mate would love Trey as much as I expected him to. I had never expressed this to Don, but he certainly exceeded my expectations. Realizing I could trust him with my child helped me let down many of my barriers.

Purchasing a new home also helped to unite us. Eight months after our wedding, Don and I both sold our houses and together we bought a new one. The search excited Trey. He ran from room to room, opening closet doors and peering into cabinets. Although it was difficult for Trey and me to leave the home we had shared for eight years, deciding on and moving into "our" home was a major bonding event.

Don's and my physical relationship has been a powerful cement in our marriage from the beginning. When we were still dating, I used to think, *I can't face the rest of my life without his kisses.* His tenderness and love as a husband make me feel secure in our relationship.

Each couple has unique events and feelings that help to merge their lives into one lane. Decide which are best for you and build on them. Look for ways to accentuate the bonding already taking place.

2. Discovered Family

Like the "microwave society" we live in, newly blended couples step into an immediate family. The adults instantly have children and children instantly have new siblings who compete for time and space. You get so tied up in disruptions, children's adjustments, demands of already existing careers, dealing with ex's, changing roles of grandparents, etc., that you relish the thought of having someone to share parenting duties.

The first little while may go smoother than expected. But suddenly, you discover that the sweet children you had before your marriage have turned into little beasties. And your partner, who perhaps has never been a parent before, cannot understand how your children can behave so badly.

On the other hand, we have seen some couples use

the dynamic of discovered family to enhance their relationship.

Our neighbor, Ken Kielbas, married for the first time at the age of 37. His new wife Betty had two children, 8 and 9. Within the first year of marriage, Ken and Betty had a baby daughter. Bachelor Ken had acquired a family with three children within one year.

His attitude is remarkable. He treats everyone in the family equally. You would not know his stepchildren are not his own unless someone told you. We tremendously admire his willingness to adjust. He deserves a medal.

My brother Jim married at age 39. His wife Denise had a 6-year-old daughter named Mandy. This was a second marriage for both of them, but Jim's first experience with a child.

Right away, Jim scheduled time for Mandy and him to share. One of the times he brought her to see us. He called me to arrange their visit, explaining he had the afternoon planned and written out.

When he arrived, he eased into a chair with a sigh. "LaDean, what do you do when plans A, B and C are all used up in the first hour, and then plans D, E and F are gone too?"

I smiled. "Welcome to the world of parenting." Then I occupied Mandy for a while to let Jim regroup.

After the two of them left, Don and I almost died laughing.

Since then, Jim and Denise have added a son to the family. Within fourteen months, Jim has become the father of two. What a great opportunity for growth!

When both partners have older children, family difficulties emerge immediately. Who has to share a room? Who decides which television show to watch? How do you share the furniture, the toys—and especially Mom's and Dad's time?

We have been talking about the children being the

discovered family, but we also must remember that our children are *discovering* family themselves at the same time. Trey, an only child, was thrown into an instant family when my ex-husband remarried. He confided in me, "My stepbrother and stepsister are using all my stuff. They have taken over my old bedroom and ride my go-cart and watch my television set every day. I only get to use my things every other weekend, and whenever I go over there, Dad never has time just for me anymore."

I hugged him and assured him his father still loved him as much as before. Don and I feel deeply for any family going through these transitions. Here are a couple of ideas that may make these adjustments easier:

Many times the absent child—the one not living in the home—feels a sense of loss because he has to share Dad's and Mom's time and because strange children are using his possessions. Giving the absent child special time alone with his parent and explaining that he doesn't have to share all of his favorite things will reassure him of his own importance. This may sound a bit selfish, but the absent child needs to feel that some things and some time are special to him just like they used to be.

Also, have Dad and his new family ask the absent child's permission to use his possessions. Adults may feel awkward asking permission from a child, but this simple action creates a feeling of self-worth and family unity in the absent child.

The stepfamily also benefits from the freedom to use certain possessions of the child without fear of reprisal, and they gain a stepsibling who does not feel as angry toward them because an atmosphere of mutual respect has been created.

Respect and closeness can also be nurtured through family traditions. Don shares how a blended family can use many kinds of customs to enrich their relationship.

Don _____

3. Different Traditions

Different, conflicting traditions can cause turmoil in a blended family. Remember our first Christmas and the argument over stringing the lights on the tree? Those kinds of scenes can easily destroy the atmosphere within a home.

In one of the Focus on the Family film series, Dr. James Dobson says that a child's self-esteem is wrapped up in family traditions. A blended family has a mix of old ones, new ones and blended ones. Some from the previous marriage no longer exist. For example, Christmas, vacations and birthdays can never be exactly as they were. At the same time, though, new traditions are being developed. Some of these are planned, others just happen. And even more are blends of the old and new.

Tradition transition is difficult. The loss of family customs and habits is the loss of family cement. Parents find themselves trying to bridge a feeling of acceptance to the blended child without losing any of the special relationship with the natural child. This can cause confusion and disharmony.

We encourage you to keep some of your older traditions. Respect each person's desire. Maybe one partner has a stronger feeling for the way things should be done. Or one part of the blended family may have many more special customs to contribute.

If a child values a tradition, consider it precious. LaDean and I didn't realize this until some time after we had been married. Meanwhile, my sons, David and Paul, had lost the traditions which included me. This affected their acceptance of our marriage. When LaDean and I realized we had not incorporated any of their previous customs into our family life, we began to do so. The effects of our omissions have taken years to repair.

To avoid this problem, teach your children that their old values are good even though relationships have changed. Help your children preserve the memories of his absent parent.

Developing new traditions is critical to the rebuilding of everyone's self-image, child and adult. We started a family-gathering dinner to celebrate birthdays. As our children get older and their lives become more involved, we find it more difficult to plan family times, but the effort is well worth it.

Other traditions we have added include the appearance of Santa on Christmas eve, telling a story called "God's Trees" at Christmas, and my recitation of "A Visit From St. Nicholas" with only the Christmas tree lights on. These have been important to our children and now, to our grandchildren.

When forming new customs, try to include part of a tradition that was precious to the child before the new marriage. This allows him to hold on to the old tradition and therefore hold on to a part of himself.

But be cautious. Taking something precious to "us" and including an "outsider" can cause bitterness, especially in older children. For instance, David would often call and ask, "Dad, can we play golf?"

Usually I would answer with, "Is it all right if Trey comes along?"

Sometimes David would pause, but he always graciously replied, "Sure, that's fine, Dad."

Many times I'm sure David wished he could have me to himself. I should have been more sensitive to his needs.

Adding old traditions can enrich family gatherings. LaDean and Trey had always hung a figure representing each of them on the Christmas tree. We found similar characters for each of my family members, and now each

Christmas our grandchildren are quick to run and find their figures on the tree.

Take time to share interests unique to the blended child that may be different from those of your natural one. I have always encouraged Trey's interest in music. Even though I coached both David and Paul, I did not try to fit Trey into the athletic mold. As his musical world expanded, I attended every function Trey was involved in. He enjoyed the attention so much that he affectionately named LaDean and me his "tag-alongs."

When blending traditions, respect the traditions of an ex-mate. This circumvents fear and prevents putting children in a competitive situation. For example, my ex-wife likes to color and hide Easter eggs for the children to seek. To keep the children and grandchildren from comparing or having to choose, we do not do Easter eggs, but give a gift to each instead. This allows our children and grandchildren to have a "special" tradition associated with each set of grandparents.

LaDean and I have found that when you blend your traditions to benefit each member of the family, your holidays and celebrations become richer. And your children learn how to compromise and respect each other's most precious memories.

LaDean
_____

4. Diverse Beliefs

Right after our wedding, Don and I discovered we had different ideas on child rearing. Don raised his sons by giving them an instruction only once before consequences. I would repeat my directions several times for Trey before taking action.

In blended marriages, families mix many diverse beliefs. Some problem areas may be child rearing, religion, husband/wife roles and commitments.

The key to harmony in blending beliefs is allowing differences to be acceptable and not necessarily changed. Giving in to a mate's desires whenever possible will help build unity.

But when you feel it important to have one policy, agree that change will be made gradually—not like Rambo. That is how Don and I handled our differences over discipline. We slowly made changes to give our three sons time to adjust.

Many couples disagree over which church to attend and how often. If that is true in your marriage, give your partner the freedom to seek God to the fullest he desires.

Expectations of husband/wife roles can also be different. Often these desires may be hard to define or to compromise. We realized this when our counselor asked us to list separately what we perceived as proper roles for husband and wife. With her help, we then discussed the items listed with an eye toward how much commitment we each could make to what the other expected.

Don

5. Dissimilar Lifestyles

When I met LaDean, I could not believe she went to the grocery store once a month. How in the world could anyone shop that infrequently and still get everything she needs?

I shopped often, sometimes even daily. That seemed so much simpler and handier.

Every time LaDean made her grocery list, I would complain, "What's taking so long? Let's just go and get a few things." She would answer, "I'm trying to stay within our budget. I can't do that the way you shop."

We argued about this for months. Then she challenged me, "Why don't you keep track of what you're spending?"

To show her I was right, I kept a ledger. One month we bought her way, the next mine. The day I totaled up the last column, I admitted, "We spent one-and-a-half times as much money shopping my way." She just smiled.

Now we go to the grocery store once a month, every month, and guess who's the biggest fan of this schedule?

I encourage you to listen to your mate's suggestions and respect her way of living. I had to learn this the hard way many times. For instance, LaDean and I argued over which brand of paper towels to buy. "These cheap towels go much further," I said. "We can almost buy two rolls for the price of yours."

"But this brand works much better. I just can't use that kind." She picked up the most expensive kind.

One day, she simply handed me one of my paper towels. "Why don't *you* clean the stove?"

I smugly began scrubbing. The towel fell to pieces. LaDean handed me her brand.

I scrubbed even harder. To my chagrin, the towel could be used again and again. I now tell people in the store which brand of paper towels to buy.

Also be willing to learn from the areas in which your mate excels. My finances were in a mess when we married. Since LaDean had hers all in order, we began to work on mine. It took several years, but she brought my credit rating to an excellent level. I am grateful to the Lord for her toughness in this area.

Accentuate the things you do alike. We have mentioned before that both LaDean and I like to cook. This has been a bonding force for us from the beginning. Many of our most playful times have been around the stove. The bonding we feel when we are creating, whether a simple omelette or a lavish Mexican meal, is more valuable than anything we could have been arguing about.

One day about twelve months into our marriage, after a heated argument, LaDean and I were in the kitchen preparing dinner. She said, "Do you realize what we are doing?"

I replied, "Yes, we are cutting up the salad."

"No," she said, "we are *both* cutting up the salad. We are doing something together."

In a lot of marriages the couples divide the duties rather than share them. For us, healing often begins in the kitchen—and sharing is a lot more fun.

6. Divided Loyalties

An old saying goes, "Blood runs thicker than water." It is true. In a blended family, this is seen when the natural parent puts allegiance for the child above his or her mate.

One couple who came to one of our conferences faced this. The husband told me with tears in his eyes, "My fifteen-year-old son came to live us some time ago. The boy rebelled against both his stepmother and me."

His wife nodded. "That extra tension almost destroyed our marriage."

"Yes," he went on. "My son repeatedly came between us. We tried everything we knew, including two professional sources, to help him accept our marriage. But he wouldn't." The man paused to compose himself. "Finally, I realized he wasn't going to change his attitude. So my wife and I agreed he would have to live elsewhere. The day he packed his room, my heart almost broke. The adjustment has been difficult for our family."

Not all divided loyalties are this difficult or have such a hard solution. But building unity out of divided loyalties will take time, effort and much prayer. Keep the future in perspective by realizing children grow up and move away. Continue to emphasize how valuable each person is to you and to the family unit.

7. Displaced Affections

Displaced affections result when someone within the family feels that another family member loves him less than he deserves. We have worked with families where a child feels Mom has chosen the new husband over him. In other situations, the parent prefers the child. One mother openly sided with her seventeen-year-old son, and her husband felt rejected. In another family, the mother had stronger feelings toward her child than her husband, but she refused to reject her mate.

If you find yourself battling displaced affections, remember that you are the adult. You can control your feelings. Do not allow competition for affection to force you to choose sides. Demonstrate your love for all those concerned. If you find yourself in this situation, a good reply is, "I love you both. I'm not the middle man."

Most important, ask God for strength and wisdom to help you through the bonding process. Your heavenly Father, the great rebuilder of marriages, is the only One who can reconstruct the broken pieces of your relationship and help you spin a thread of strong love between you. We suggest you set a specific time to pray as a couple. If you have achieved some success in bonding, ask Him to enrich what you already have. Your spiritual relationship will help you and your mate travel down the same road together while you build a relationship that sizzles.

MAKING OF A MIRACLE

How far have you and your partner traveled toward bonding and intimacy? We have developed a quick quiz that you can take together to help evaluate where you are on your journey. As you discuss your responses, determine where you would like to be in a month, a year or on your next milestone anniversary. Then chart a course for your destination.

An Intimate Inquiry

1. To me intimacy means:

   ❑ goal sharing
   ❑ closeness
   ❑ sex
   ❑ parenthood

2. I feel intimate when . . .

   ❑ . . . we share private thoughts.
   ❑ . . . we go for a walk.
   ❑ . . . we touch.
   ❑ . . . we talk about our time away from each other.
   ❑ . . . we share a project.

3. Intimacy is difficult when . . .

   ❑ . . . I am tired.
   ❑ . . . I am rushed for time.
   ❑ . . . I fear what you will do with my vulnerability.
   ❑ . . . I am not sure how you feel.

4. I could become more intimate by . . .

   ❑ . . . sharing my heart when I feel hurt.
   ❑ . . . sharing my heart when I feel happy.
   ❑ . . . sharing my future dreams and/or my past.
   ❑ . . . sharing romantic thoughts and moments.
   ❑ . . . sharing what God is doing in my life.

We suggest you set a time for a date with your mate. Take this opportunity to arrange a weekend alone at the lake, a night in a hotel or a romantic dinner for two to discuss your Intimate Inquiry.

6

One Nail at a Time

LaDean

Several years before I met Don, my previous marriage was in trouble. One morning, I awoke to find a gun on the floor. "Why is that here?" I asked my husband.

He just shrugged.

As I crawled out of bed, my thoughts began to whirl. *Did he hear something during the night? What if Trey would happen to find it?* I pictured our little son coming into the bedroom late at night and picking up the weapon. Many times I had read in the newspaper of this happening. But I dismissed my fears as too dramatic.

After several mornings of finding the gun on the floor, I began to realize my fears were not groundless. "Honey, won't you please put that gun away?" I pleaded.

"Sure," he agreed, but the next morning it was again on the floor beside the bed.

This continued for many months. One morning I awoke to find the gun between us in bed. I asked what it was doing there and my husband told me he had heard something during the night.

Morning after morning, I awoke to the same fearful

scene. At first, I was irritated. Then my anger turned to fear. Finally, I decided to dismiss the whole thing from my mind. This reality denial worked. I went back to my daily roles of mothering, teaching and befriending as if nothing unusual were happening.

Then one morning, the gun between us was pointed at me. I was immobilized with fear. *What if I wake up dead? Maybe I should tell someone. But who would believe me?* I could hardly believe it myself, and I was living it.

For the next few days, I pretended to sleep at night but laid awake too terrified to close my eyes. *What's wrong with me? I know things will work out. Thank goodness it's summer now, and I don't have to go to work.*

Soon I was afraid to close my eyes in my house, even during the day. After several days and nights without sleep, I would take Trey to my parents' home and tell my mother, "I don't feel too good. Will you watch Trey while I lie down?"

After a few times, she began to question me, "La-Dean, what's wrong?"

I couldn't tell her the truth so I took Trey to my closest friend, Ila. I would say something like, "I've been working late on a project, and I need some sleep. Could you watch Trey?" Then I would take a nap at her place.

Finally, I broke down and confided in her. "Have you told your psychologist about this?" she asked. Can you believe we had been seeing a marriage counselor for a year and I had never mentioned this to him?

I shook my head.

"Call him right now," Ila insisted.

I did, and he told me to get the guns out of the house. He said that in situations like this, the people involved can be suicidal as well as homicidal. According to the Fort Worth *Star Telegram* of January 21, 1990, in 1989 in Tarrant County, Texas, of 139 homicides, 39 were a result of domestic violence. Had I been aware of these statistics regarding domestic violence, I'm sure I would have taken action more quickly.

In the six months that followed, I prayed every time I left the counselor's office. If I had ever entertained thoughts of suicide, this certainly would have cured them. It made me realize I did not want to die. I wanted life, even if it was not the life I had planned. This taught me to survive tough times, and it was the beginning of my reaffirming the values I had lost or compromised. I had not been close to the Lord for a long time, but at this time He definitely became my help in time of need.

It took me an additional six months of counseling and personal growth to become strong enough to face the reality that my marriage was hopeless—there was a lot more involved than just the gun incident.

I finally left the relationship behind, but I brought with me the fears, guilt and unresolved feelings of the past. I still held resentment toward my ex-husband.

The Process of Forgiveness

Forgiveness is one of the most complex and difficult actions in life because it touches the most tender part of our beings. Yet the Bible commands us to forgive completely and unconditionally—as God forgives (Matthew 6:14,15).

Making this work in everyday experience is difficult. Unforgiveness is one of the greatest causes of broken relationships, broken marriages and broken families. Harboring grudges and past hurts leads to cynical attitudes, hostility, anger, self-pity and eventually to bitterness. The root of this bitterness produces a tree of sarcastic, negative, judgmental and controlling attitudes which shadow every part of our lives.

Forgiveness is probably one of the most important principles for blended families because of the effect of unforgiveness on every other aspect of family life. A widow or widower entering a blended family, for example, must deal with feelings of anger toward the deceased spouse for leaving him or her. Many times the most difficult hurdle is for those who experience a failed marriage. If we harbor unforgiveness toward our former partner, it will be carried over to the new marriage.

That is what happened to me. I concealed my feelings of anger and hate, and they affected my relationship with Don.

When Don and I were about to give up on the war we called our marriage, our counselor, Brooke Annis, told us, "You'll have to get off your mountains of unforgiveness or your relationship won't make it."

I looked at Don. Life had not turned out like I had planned, and I blamed him for much of my disappointments. I was "keeping score" of past hurts and pains, piling up ammunition for the next battle. And I still clung to my resentments from the past.

I swallowed hard. *I'll have to admit I was wrong,* I thought. It was a hard step to take—but I agreed. Don had to take the same step.

Since then, Don and I have seen forgiveness blossom in our lives, but learning to forgive has been both frustrating and freeing. In order to accomplish it, we have found it necessary to go through a process that involves the following five steps, and we trust that applying these steps will bring you freedom and hope as it has us.

1. Recognize the Situation, Source and Solution

This step involves three parts.

First, *recognize the situation.* In my case, to heal the bitterness I felt toward my ex-husband, I had to admit my contribution to the break-up of our relationship. I had to determine what I was doing or not doing that caused me not to forgive him or myself. Because of some of the choices I had made, I had nurtured an abusive marriage. When I confessed that, I felt overwhelmed.

I remember thinking, *I could have behaved differently. If I had, perhaps the results would have been different, too.*

I recounted all that I had experienced and how it affected my present relationships. Then healing began. Now I realize that if I had not faced my situation, Don and I could not have bonded.

Sometimes we find it easier to forgive others than to forgive ourselves. An unforgiving attitude toward yourself only leads to a lack of self-esteem and despair. On the other hand, forgiving yourself lifts a great burden from your shoulders that you may have been carrying for years.

Second, *recognize the source of your forgiveness—* God's grace. True forgiveness comes from the Lord. We are not naturally forgiving beings, and we need the power that He gives to resolve our bitter feelings against others.

Third, the solution is to *take responsibility for working out forgiveness* in everyday life. That was the most difficult part for me. The day-to-day practicalities of forgiving myself and others took much prayer and commitment.

Don, too, had his struggles with forgiving. He had to deal with his attitude toward his parents.

Don

My first step was to recognize the anger I felt toward my mother and father for creating codependency in me. Don the Perfect had to open his eyes to the truth. I didn't want to sugar-coat anything. I wanted freedom from my past.

First, I admitted that I had been Mother's preacher-boy and Dad's athlete. I had to recognize that they felt I was the only one who could solve their problems.

Then I had to admit that this codependence had contributed to my divorce and was causing stress in my new marriage. I had to accept the fact that I was not responsible for everyone else's life.

To begin the process, I needed the help of a friend. Lana Bateman forced me to look at some issues and situations I had pretended did not exist. She told me, "You are forty-eight and you have been married to La-Dean for six years. Isn't it time you took a look at the real Don Houck?"

Finally, Don the Perfect had to admit that he wasn't so perfect after all, and that he didn't have the answers to everyone's problems.

We encourage you to take this first step to forgiveness. Ask God to help you look at your situation through His eyes. Rely on His strength to help you apply these principles in your life.

But this is just the beginning. LaDean has an amazing story about how she learned to release the pain of her experience.

LaDean
_____

2. Release the Hold that Defeat, Pain and Anger Have on You

Don and I have discovered that the terrible trio of defeat, pain and anger make up a black cloud of guilt. It not only destroys relationships but also self-esteem. Yet most blended partners find it difficult to recognize the source of their guilt. Often we accept God's forgiveness but don't forgive ourselves. Or we pass our guilt from a divorce onto our children, so we don't discipline properly and that causes insecurity in them. Many times we also transfer our feelings of guilt onto our new partner.

Both Don and I have made great progress in releasing our guilt. Only in the past year, however, have I been able to recount the episode with the gun in my former marriage without a pounding heart, shallow breathing and shaking hands. Trey was the one who helped me release my pain.

One day I was typing the account when he walked into my study. "What are you writing, Mom?" he asked me.

"About an incident with your father. The gun story."

"What's the gun story about? Can I read it?"

I was face to face with what I suddenly realized was my greatest fear: what Trey would think of me and his father when he knew the truth. I gathered myself together as best I could and sighed, "No, I need to tell you this one."

With sweaty hands, I related how his father had put a gun between us in bed. I described my fears, and how I hid the truth from everyone for years.

"Boy, you guys were weird." He shook his head.

His acceptance of his father and me, and of my feelings, relieved my mind tremendously.

As we talked, I even shared some of my weaknesses and how I contributed to the situation. Our conversation brought us closer together by opening up communication about the past, and it helped him understand some of the actions I took when he was a boy. I recognized that God had laid the groundwork and engineered the timing and circumstances to prepare both Trey and me for when this had to happen. Telling Trey helped me deal with a lot of the guilt I had concealed. I also recognized how far the Lord had brought all of us in healing and loving.

I can find some humor in nearly every situation, but I never have been able to laugh about any part of this one. It was just too serious. The experience of just telling it was a trauma for me. But with God's help, we made it and it has been beneficial for all of us.

Releasing comes through physical, mental and spiritual preparation. Physical preparation is seeing the situation as it is. Mental preparation is making a choice about how to deal with the problem and its effect. And spiritual preparation is searching the Scriptures and calling on God to strengthen you as you carry out the proper response.

Don and I consciously follow this process every time a hurtful incident occurs in our relationship. We use Matthew 18:22 to help us remember that the Lord expects us to forgive seventy times seven. Sometimes we talk through how to put our guilt and anger into perspective so we can release the unforgiveness.

This process also worked in my relationship with my ex-husband. I had prayed about his attitude and mine for months. Because of my apprehensions, I delayed writing about the incident with the gun until the last possible moment. Then one night I asked him to look over the account as I had written it and sign a release so I could print it in this book.

I felt tense as he began to read.

Finally, he looked up. "I'm so sorry. I had no idea. I would never have done anything to hurt you or Trey." He then repeated this to Trey and apologized to both of us several times.

Suddenly, I realized how much I had grown through this incident. I reassured him, "Don't feel badly. Because of this situation and others, I am different. And I like the 'me' I am now much better than the 'me' I was then."

For me, forgiveness has been and still is a process. I had forgiven my ex-husband in stages for various things, but talking over the incident with Trey and then with my ex-husband allowed me to release the pain and guilt, and it was an exercise in true forgiveness. I realized the grace of God was responsible for the restored relationship with my ex-husband. I also forgave myself for what Trey had lost in the break-up of his family.

But more important, the Lord used this opportunity to help me grow, develop, toughen and yet soften, and to bring me closer to Him.

Don

Restitution is an important part of releasing. Restitution is a "pay-back" and it contains two components: the negative is compensation and the positive is restoration. Compensation is a way of "making up for the damage" out of guilt. We may compensate for a break up in our marriage by overachieving at work, relaxing discipline with our children or giving excessive amounts of money to an absent child. In this way we try to repair the destruction brought about in our lives and in the lives of family and friends.

We move from compensation to restoration (a healthy approach to restoring the damage done) by learning to correct the destructive behavior we see in ourselves. This is where we find release.

We begin restoration by changing our focus on life situations. Some circumstances we can control; others we cannot. But we can decide how to view our situation. As we move toward restoration, we give our relationship the release and freedom it must have in order to grow and develop.

LaDean

3. Review Your Attitude, Actions and Associations

Reviewing is the process of dealing with the past as it is brought to our minds. Simply ask yourself, "How do

I feel about this circumstance? What will I allow it to do in my life?"

Reviewing is not reliving. Sometimes in reliving we reclaim the old pain. In reviewing, we formulate new thoughts and feelings. We have to be teachable. Use review as a spiritual check to make sure you are still in God's will.

For instance, I had been going over and over the gun story in my mind for years. That was not healthy. In writing about my feelings, I was able to focus on rectifying the situation for everyone involved. Then I could begin forgiving.

4. Rejoice in the Grace of God

The Lord, through His gentle Spirit, desires to build strength in us and help us grow through overcoming. He encourages us to have joy in this process. First Peter 1:6,7 says:

> In this you greatly rejoice, even though now for a little while, if necessary, you have been distressed by various trials, that the proof of your faith, being more precious than gold which is perishable, even though tested by fire, may be found to result in praise and glory and honor at the revelation of Jesus Christ (NAS).

This is where theology became reality for me. Growth means change, sometimes expanding our focus, sometimes stretching our reach. Growth also means we do something—we do not stand still.

Growth brings joy. I experienced this process when I returned to my former school to teach an in-service workshop. Some of my friends commented that I was not the LaDean they had known before. I was not arrogant and insecure but confident and pleased about my life. What joy to know that others could see the change in me! I was reminded how much the Lord had built into my character through my past.

Maybe you have experienced the separation of friends or the trauma of divorce. Growing through these devastations can be extremely painful. In time your change may become uncomfortable for your friends, especially if they have chosen to stay where they are. Some may decide to turn their backs on you. Despite the cost, we must continue learning and changing and rejoicing in the Lord for what He is doing in our life.

Every time God does something for His people, they celebrate. Sometimes a celebration is a smile from our heart, a squeeze of a hand, a shout to the Lord, a song given to Him or a special evening. Sometimes it is sharing His mercy and grace with other people. Some of us have to give ourselves permission to celebrate life, even life in Christ. As we work through this rejoicing process, we can learn to celebrate.

We have one more step to complete the process of forgiveness. Don has struggled in this area, and he shares his story.

Don

5. Relax by Resting in God

LaDean and I use a phrase that Patsy Clairmont, a friend of ours and author of *God Uses Cracked Pots,* gave us: "That's life; get on the bus." To us, this means to quit dwelling on what you can't change and get on with life. A sense of humor really helps. Let me illustrate.

It's impossible to start the day on the right foot when you only have left shoes. Don't laugh. That happened to me.

One morning I sat on my bed looking into my closet. All I could see were left shoes. Where had all the right ones gone?

Immediately, anger and frustration burned in my

heart. I felt my ex-wife had done this, but *why would she do such a thing?*

I had been letting everyone know how unfair life was to poor me. The bitterness was about to eat me up. And now this!

Suddenly, God spoke to me in the quietness of my heart, and I saw the humor. Laughing, I said, "You guys look like me—all alone and on the wrong foot." I even felt a bit of jealousy that I had not thought of it first—all those left shoes, standing in a row!

The right shoes had disappeared—and I never did find them!

None of us can forgive without God's help. We have to rely on Him to help us accept our reality, to remove our feelings of defeat, pain and anger, and to rest in Him.

We begin by asking Jesus to be in control of our life and marriage. Then we can consciously work to "take each thought captive unto the obedience of Christ" (2 Corinthians 10:5, NAS). This requires action, not just thoughts or plans. Ask Him to help you forgive your former spouse of the things he or she has done that cause you bitterness and anger. Identify these feelings by name, and ask the Lord to forgive you for harboring them. True forgiveness does not mean you will never remember the incident, just that your reaction is godly and under control.

Sometimes a sense of humor can be the vehicle to help you relax, to have the freedom to go on living. I don't believe God wants us to handle everything with a joke, but when circumstances are completely out of your control, a laugh can be your statement that anger and bitterness are not going to rule your life. This can give you the courage to let God control the situation.

The farther I am from the day I could only find left shoes, the funnier it seems. This story has become a symbol of how God can help me see the lighter side of my problems.

Take Out One Nail at a Time

I once heard a story about a wise father who taught his son a valuable lesson as the boy was growing up. Each time the son required discipline, the father sent him to the backyard to drive a nail into a post the father had placed there. After a number of years, the post was full of nails.

In young manhood, the son's behavior became more positive. Each time he made a mature choice, he was allowed to remove one nail. Just before leaving home, he finally yanked out the last one.

The proud father threw a great celebration. During the festivities, the son pointed to the post and said to his dad, "I'm really pleased that I was able to remove all the nails, but I feel sad that the post is full of holes."

The wise father replied, "Don't feel bad. Those holes are just scars of the good lessons you have learned from the poor choices you made."

He put his arm around his son. "In life, many times we have to overcome the effects of our poor choices, but the scars from those choices often remain a part of us.

"When we sin," the father explained, "God forgives us. But marks are left to remind us of the great freedom and forgiveness He has given us. We are not to dwell on the scars or on their past pain, but we are to remember that our choices can bring us unhappiness or joy."

Unforgiveness will cause great holes in our lives, but as we forgive both ourselves and others, the wounds will heal and only the scars will remain. We can use those reminders of the past to keep fresh the joy and growth we have experienced through the power of forgiveness.

MAKING OF A MIRACLE

At this point we would encourage you, as a couple, to share what God has revealed to you as you have read this chapter. Accepting the forgiveness of God begins your process of forgiving yourself and others. This represents the strength we have in Christ.

The "Blend Card" you'll find at the end of this and each of the following chapters is important to your journey. Use these cards, write on them, carry them with you as a focus of concentration for positive thoughts and communication with your mate. Record on your "Blessing Card" the blessings you receive, beginning with a positive characteristic of your mate.

After carrying them for a week, put them on a key ring to remind you of their message. Keep them close by the telephone, your car radio or on your dressing table to give you a needed lift during your day. We call this ring of cards a strength circle because it represents the strength God gives us through His never-ending love.

Blend for the week of _____

God's greatest gift is His forgiveness of our sins. His second greatest gift is giving us the capacity to forgive ourselves and others.

> *Then I will make up to you for the years*
> *that the swarming locust has eaten.*
> (Joel 2:25, NAS)

Blessings for the week of _____

7

The Real You

Don

When we first married, I decided LaDean's self-image needed my help. So I enrolled her in a Mary Kay cosmetics course and began looking for other ways to make her sparkle.

I bought several books on wardrobe planning. In the back of one, *Shades of Beauty* by Marita Littauer, I found an address for a week-long seminar on how to do color analysis. *Just what LaDean needs*, I decided.

I had her sign a letter I had written requesting information, and I mailed it. A few days later, an application arrived.

As part of the registration requirements, LaDean had to fill out a personality profile. The instructors used the information to find out if the student had the right personality to do color analysis and to match her up with a compatible roommate. LaDean filled in the blanks and sent in the application.

LaDean

I was happy Don did this. I would never have done it myself—my self-image was too poor. In June I prepared to fly to California for the week of training. On the way to the airport, Don and I had another of our screaming "discussions." I am sure those who have experienced a screaming discussion know exactly what I mean.

When I met my roommate for the week, we were like long-lost high school friends. We stayed up late the first night talking. Right then, I decided that the personality profile must have some value.

Marita Littauer and her mother, Florence, taught the sessions. Florence introduced us to temperaments which we will discuss a little later in this chapter.

Don called me during the week.

"You won't believe the wonderful concepts we're learning!" I exclaimed. "I can hardly wait to tell you about them." Secretly, I was thinking, *This will help straighten you out!*

Don and Trey drove to California to pick me up after the color analysis school so we could vacation for two weeks. As we left, I suggested, "Don, let's listen to Florence's tapes."

"I don't want to," he replied firmly.

After a few hundred more miles, I said again, "Don, let's listen to Florence's tapes."

Again he said, "I don't want to."

Some more miles and I asked him again, and he said, "Oh, okay, on one condition."

"What's that?"

"That you shut up!"

I didn't think that was very nice, but . . . whatever it takes! So we began to listen to the tapes. Trey must have been glad we decided to listen to something because we had been arguing about everything. He had escaped into sleep a lot in the back seat and by now had plugged his ears with his Walkman.

As Florence began describing the temperaments, I kept glancing at Don to see if he was getting the message. He needed to change his behavior. Then slowly the truth from Florence's talk began to seep into my head. The problem with us was not so much Don as it was me. Don later told me that he too got the message. He felt the problem with us was him.

After listening for a long time, I began to feel tired. My head nodded, and I fell sound asleep.

Suddenly, I awoke to the twisting and turning of the car making hairpin turns on a narrow road. The tires rattled over gravel instead of pavement. Then the gravel ended, and the road became a dirt trail.

"Where are we?" I demanded.

"I took a short cut to Carmel," Don said sheepishly.

Since I am not a country girl, being there made me nervous. In fact, if I had not been so frightened, I would have gotten out of the car right then.

"I hope we find a gas station soon," Don muttered anxiously.

I couldn't believe it! All I could see were trees and cows and an occasional house. There were no gas stations out here.

Trey's shaky voice piped up from the back seat. "I don't feel so good."

I added my two cents' worth. "Now that I think about it, I don't feel too good either."

"Neither do I," Don admitted.

Then I said something really helpful. "You've made all of us carsick by taking this stupid road you call a shortcut! We're about to run out of gas, and it's almost dark. No one will ever find us out here."

Don didn't answer.

"Why did I ever come on vacation with you? If I had enough money and could find an airport, I would fly home, and you could fall off the edge of the ocean—if you could find it!"

Around the next curve, we saw a small town with paved streets and a gas station.

Don breathed a sigh of relief. "This is an answer to a 'fervent prayer.' " I wasn't in the mood for theology, but I did appreciate God "answering the prayer of a fool."

After filling the gas tank, we continued on our not-so-delightful vacation. Don later told me that by the time we started back toward Texas, he had decided to get a divorce. This marriage wasn't going to last long. He pondered his decision all the way across Arizona and New Mexico.

Florence's testimony of how understanding temperaments can change lives haunted him, though. Finally, he decided he would give our marriage another six months.

Back home, both of us began applying many of the principles we had learned. By the end of the six months, Don had experienced such a change in himself that the deadline was forgotten. The understanding of temperaments did not provide a quick fix for our marriage, but it did give us a foundation from which to work.

The Difference Between You and Me

We wish we could take credit for discovering and developing these concepts, but we cannot. We're indebted to Florence Littauer and what we have learned from her seminars, books and cassette tapes for the information we'll be sharing on the personality types.

In about 400 B.C., Hippocrates, a Greek physician, developed the theory of temperaments. He said all people can be grouped into one of four basic personality groups: sanguine, choleric, melancholy and phlegmatic. Each person predominantly falls into one of the four categories but has secondary traits from another as well.

Each of us has a unique combination of these personality traits which makes us act the way we do. When we understand the characteristics common to the temperament of our spouse or closest friends, we can see how they differ from us and we can handle the differences easier. Three essential guidelines help us deal with dissimilarities between ourselves and others.

First, *being different is not wrong.* It is not my job to change my spouse, only to understand him.

When Don and I first married, our arguments would end with his conceding, "Well, you're just different from me."

I would answer, "Yes, we're different. And I don't care if you aren't just like me." But deep down, I did care. If Don would just act and think like me, want the same things I did, and react like I did, my life would be a lot simpler. But I know now, it would be *boring!*

One of my choleric characteristics is a desire to remake everyone, so this concept became very important to me: "It is not my job to change you." I found that remaking people is a heavy burden to carry. How much wiser to let Don be Don and LaDean be LaDean.

Second, *any strength carried to an extreme becomes a weakness.* For example, if you are a perfectionist, you probably do a good job at keeping your home clean. But your drive can also cause you to be critical of someone who messes up your territory. As we describe the four temperaments and how they interact, I think you will be able to see how this principle works.

Third, *I must first know myself before I can understand others or be of help to anyone else.* Since I began to understand myself, I have been able to handle the conflicts in my life more successfully. Accepting my own strengths and weaknesses helps me accept others as they are.

By now you must be wondering exactly how you can recognize these temperaments. We would like to give you a simple sketch of each one. We'll begin with the two extroverts, sanguine and choleric, and then describe the two introverts, melancholy and phlegmatic.

Sanguine

Basic motivation: "Let's have fun."

Character traits	Body language
Eternal optimist who sees life through rose-colored glasses	Demonstrative gestures
Lives in the present, the here and now, enjoys whatever he is doing	Springy "cheerleader" walk
Decisions based on feelings rather than logic	Wears flamboyant clothing in both design and color
Encourages others	Happy-go-lucky
Quick to forgive because he doesn't always remember what he has done, doesn't carry a grudge	Holds onto another person when talking to him
Tells good stories but exaggerates details, loves to talk	Wide-open eyes

Some friends of ours, Billy and Cheryl Stewart, have two precious sons. One, Chas, is a sanguine. In the first grade, he had difficulty staying in his chair and not talking. His parents tried every form of encouragement to correct this behavior. But he continued to get poor conduct marks on his report card.

On the way to school one morning, Cheryl and Chas had a "talk" and she encouraged him to stay at his desk. After every block or two she would say, "Chas, what are you going to do today?"

"I'm not going to get out of my chair, and I'm not going to talk out of turn."

This exchange went on all the way to school.

When Cheryl picked him up after school, he waved a note from his teacher telling how well he had behaved. Cheryl said enthusiastically, "I'm so proud of you, Chas. I'm going to buy you some ice cream now and fix your favorite meal tonight. We're going to celebrate." She knew a sanguine thrives on praise.

When they got home, she emptied his lunch box. The only item missing was his juice. She called him into the kitchen. "Chas, why didn't you eat the rest of your lunch?"

"Mom, I didn't have time. Lunch was the only time I could talk."

His mother smiled. He was beginning to learn how to compensate for his strength carried to an extreme.

Choleric

Basic motivation: "Do it my way, now!"

Character Traits	Body Language
Primary goal is accomplishment	Deliberate walk and gestures
Desires productivity over sensitivity	Hard heel-toe walk
Believes his instructions should be followed immediately	Stands with weight evenly distributed
Tends to be unsympathetic	Stands with both hands on his hips when angry
Finds it difficult to apologize	When talking, one hand will be on his hip while the other is either clenched or has the index finger pointed
Excels in emergencies	Territorial actions
Organized but uses his own method of arranging his possessions	Reacts coolly in emergencies and crises

| Self-centered but the most receptive to changing the way he thinks, feels and reacts | Often has dramatic, piercing eyes that stare right through you |

I had a student several years ago whose boyfriend was killed because of mistaken identity. When we studied temperaments the next year, I explained to the class, "Cholerics do not like tears because they think crying is a sign of weakness."

Afterward, she rushed up to me. "Mrs. Houck, you mean I'm not crazy?"

I was mystified. "Why are you asking me about being crazy?"

"I have not cried since my boyfriend's death. I miss him, and I ache for him. But I have not cried. I thought there was something wrong with me."

I asked her what she had done since the tragedy, and she described how she had gone from one project to another to another.

Work is often the choleric's answer to emotional stress.

Her response made me remember how I had reacted when my first marriage was falling apart. My husband and I were not communicating. Since he didn't come home until late every night, I immersed myself in cleaning. Having a spotless house was the only part of my life I thought I could control.

Melancholy

Basic motivation: "If it's worth doing, do it right."

Character traits	Body language
Perfectionist, including clothing and grooming	Stands with weight on one foot with hands clasped in front of self in "fig leaf" position

Organized	Gestures close to body
The most artistic, creative, musical, poetic and cultured of all the temperaments	As he walks, he heel-toes one foot and drags the other heel
Intelligent	Feels more secure if he touches an object or leans against a wall or cabinet with the upper part of his leg
Sensitive	Appears serious because he looks down
Arrives early for appointments because he is so aware of other people's time	Is depressed when he fails his own high standards
Accurate with facts and figures, good money manager	Seeks approval

When I teach temperaments in my high school classroom, I select four administrators as examples. I ask them to come into my room and talk to my students. When the administrators leave, the students and I discuss the character traits they noticed.

One of my favorite administrators, Jimmy Jones, used to stand in a perfect "fig leaf" position. Word got back to him how we had described his stance.

"Fig leaf!" he declared. "I'll never be your melancholy again."

The next year, when he stood in front of the students, he clasped his hands behind his back. Although this posture normally represents openness, my students immediately recognized that Jimmy was consciously avoiding the fig leaf position. He didn't have any of them fooled.

Phlegmatic

Basic motivation: "Don't get too involved. Do it the easy way."

Character Traits	Body Language
Easy going and laid back, creates and seeks peace	Stands with weight on one foot and hands in pocket jingling change, or with arms crossed over chest
Consistent, secure, comfortable	When sitting, he scoots down and crosses his arms and legs
Normally a background person but will excel in a position of leadership because he guides rather than orders	When walking, he turns his feet out and shuffles along
Allows those with whom he works the freedom to do a job without constant supervision	Watches rather than participates
Great listener but a reluctant communicator	Shows little expression
Makes friends easily	Holds back on sharing thoughts and feelings
Good counselor	Will go along with whatever anyone suggests
Accepts you as you are	

Don's brother, Jim, is the perfect example of a phlegmatic, who is the world's natural tranquilizer, creating and seeking peace.

As a police detective, he sometimes works with the sexual assault unit. Our neighbor who works with the Department of Human Services told us that when an abused child arrives at the hospital, authorities often request Jim's help in taking the offense report from the child. His gestures are close body; he talks slowly in a low voice; and his movements are non-threatening. Since he doesn't intimidate the victim, he has an ability to get information from a frightened child without causing additional trauma.

If you ask a phlegmatic what he would like to do or where he would like to go and he tells you he doesn't care, believe him. It really doesn't matter much to him. He will have a great time if you just plan the event, and then grab him by the hand and go.

Do these charts and examples give you an idea of what each temperament is like? At the end of this chapter, we have included a Personality Profile from Florence Littauer's book, *Personality Plus* for your own personality analysis.[1] Take the time now to fill in the profile and complete the scoring sheet before you continue reading. The information will give you a clearer insight into why you act and react the way you do.

Each of us has unique ways of expressing our temperaments. Sometimes, we cover up some of the traits that make us feel uncomfortable. Other times, we have difficulty understanding the complex natures of our partner or children.

In the next chapter, we want to explore special complexities in temperament analysis that will help uncover personality traits hidden beneath the surface. By learning to express your true self and understanding your mate's behavior, you will find greater freedom in your relationship.

MAKING OF A MIRACLE

After working through the profile in this chapter, we suggest you set a time for another date with your mate.

The first assignment for each of you is to share what you feel your three greatest strengths are, and the three characteristics you would most like to change. As your mate shares his or hers with you, your function is to listen and receive without judging. This is a good time to develop a plan of action for change, and to commit to support and encourage each other in your attempts to make these changes. Allow time for gentle prayer and take these concerns to the Lord.

The second part of this assignment is to share with each other what characteristic of your mate's is most exciting to you. We pray for you as you begin to experience healing and joy. Allow the verse on the Blend Card for this chapter to inspire you to be transparent with each other.

Blend for the week of _____

Just because you are different doesn't make you wrong. It is not my job to change your temperament, only to understand it.

Therefore, confess your sins to one another, and pray for one another, so that you may be healed. The effective prayer of a righteous man can accomplish much.
(James 5:16, NAS)

Blessings for the week of _____

Personality Profile

DIRECTIONS — In each of the following rows of four words across, place an X in front of the one word that most often applies to you. Continue through all forty lines. Be sure each number is marked. If you are not sure of which word "most applies", ask a spouse or a friend.

STRENGTHS

1	___ Adventurous	___ Adaptable	___ Animated	___ Analytical
2	___ Persistent	___ Playful	___ Persuasive	___ Peaceful
3	___ Submissive	___ Self-sacrificing	___ Sociable	___ Strong-willed
4	___ Considerate	___ Controlled	___ Competitive	___ Convincing
5	___ Refreshing	___ Respectful	___ Reserved	___ Resourceful
6	___ Satisfied	___ Sensitive	___ Self-reliant	___ Spirited
7	___ Planner	___ Patient	___ Positive	___ Promoter
8	___ Sure	___ Spontaneous	___ Scheduled	___ Shy
9	___ Orderly	___ Obliging	___ Outspoken	___ Optimistic
10	___ Friendly	___ Faithful	___ Funny	___ Forceful
11	___ Daring	___ Delightful	___ Diplomatic	___ Detailed
12	___ Cheerful	___ Consistent	___ Cultured	___ Confident
13	___ Idealistic	___ Independent	___ Inoffensive	___ Inspiring
14	___ Demonstrative	___ Decisive	___ Dry humor	___ Deep
15	___ Mediator	___ Musical	___ Mover	___ Mixes easily
16	___ Thoughtful	___ Tenacious	___ Talker	___ Tolerant
17	___ Listener	___ Loyal	___ Leader	___ Lively
18	___ Contented	___ Chief	___ Chartmaker	___ Cute
19	___ Perfectionist	___ Pleasant	___ Productive	___ Popular
20	___ Bouncy	___ Bold	___ Behaved	___ Balanced

Personality Profile

21	____ Blank	____ Bashful	____ Brassy	____ Bossy
22	____ Undisciplined	____ Unsympathetic	____ Unenthusiastic	____ Unforgiving
23	____ Reticent	____ Resentful	____ Resistant	____ Repetitious
24	____ Fussy	____ Fearful	____ Forgetful	____ Frank
25	____ Impatient	____ Insecure	____ Indecisive	____ Interrupts
26	____ Unpopular	____ Uninvolved	____ Unpredictable	____ Unaffectionate
27	____ Headstrong	____ Haphazard	____ Hard to please	____ Hesitant
28	____ Plain	____ Pessimistic	____ Proud	____ Permissive
29	____ Angered easily	____ Aimless	____ Argumentative	____ Alienated
30	____ Naive	____ Negative attitude	____ Nervy	____ Nonchalant
31	____ Worrier	____ Withdrawn	____ Workaholic	____ Wants credit
32	____ Too sensitive	____ Tactless	____ Timid	____ Talkative
33	____ Doubtful	____ Disorganized	____ Domineering	____ Depressed
34	____ Inconsistent	____ Introvert	____ Intolerant	____ Indifferent
35	____ Messy	____ Moody	____ Mumbles	____ Manipulative
36	____ Slow	____ Stubborn	____ Show-off	____ Skeptical
37	____ Loner	____ Lord over	____ Lazy	____ Loud
38	____ Sluggish	____ Suspicious	____ Short-tempered	____ Scatterbrained
39	____ Revengeful	____ Restless	____ Reluctant	____ Rash
40	____ Compromising	____ Critical	____ Crafty	____ Changeable

NOW TRANSFER ALL YOUR X's TO THE CORRESPONDING WORDS ON THE PERSONALITY SCORING SHEET AND ADD UP YOUR TOTALS.

Personality Scoring Sheet

STRENGTHS

	SANGUINE POPULAR	CHOLERIC POWERFUL	MELANCHOLY PERFECT	PHLEGMATIC PEACEFUL
1	Animated	Adventurous	Analytical	Adaptable
2	Playful	Persuasive	Persistent	Peaceful
3	Sociable	Strong-willed	Self-sacrificing	Submissive
4	Convincing	Competitive	Considerate	Controlled
5	Refreshing	Resourceful	Respectful	Reserved
6	Spirited	Self-reliant	Sensitive	Satisfied
7	Promoter	Positive	Planner	Patient
8	Spontaneous	Sure	Scheduled	Shy
9	Optimistic	Outspoken	Orderly	Obliging
10	Funny	Forceful	Faithful	Friendly
11	Delightful	Daring	Detailed	Diplomatic
12	Cheerful	Confident	Cultured	Consistent
13	Inspiring	Independent	Idealistic	Inoffensive
14	Demonstrative	Decisive	Deep	Dry humor
15	Mixes easily	Mover	Musical	Mediator
16	Talker	Tenacious	Thoughtful	Tolerant
17	Lively	Leader	Loyal	Listener
18	Cute	Chief	Chartmaker	Contented
19	Popular	Productive	Perfectionist	Pleasant
20	Bouncy	Bold	Behaved	Balanced
TOTALS				

Personality Scoring Sheet

WEAKNESSES

	SANGUINE POPULAR	CHOLERIC POWERFUL	MELANCHOLY PERFECT	PHLEGMATIC PEACEFUL
21	Brassy	Bossy	Bashful	Blank
22	Undisciplined	Unsympathetic	Unforgiving	Unenthusiastic
23	Repetitious	Resistant	Resentful	Reticent
24	Forgetful	Frank	Fussy	Fearful
25	Interrupts	Impatient	Insecure	Indecisive
26	Unpredictable	Unaffectionate	Unpopular	Uninvolved
27	Haphazard	Headstrong	Hard-to-please	Hesitant
28	Permissive	Proud	Pessimistic	Plain
29	Angered easily	Argumentative	Alienated	Aimless
30	Naive	Nervy	Negative attitude	Nonchalant
31	Wants credit	Workaholic	Withdrawn	Worrier
32	Talkative	Tactless	Too sensitive	Timid
33	Disorganized	Domineering	Depressed	Doubtful
34	Inconsistent	Intolerant	Introvert	Indifferent
35	Messy	Manipulative	Moody	Mumbles
36	Show-off	Stubborn	Skeptical	Slow
37	Loud	Lord-over-others	Loner	Lazy
38	Scatterbrained	Short tempered	Suspicious	Sluggish
39	Restless	Rash	Revengeful	Reluctant
40	Changeable	Crafty	Critical	Compromising
TOTALS				
COMBINED TOTALS				

8

Expressing Your True Self

Don

My son, David, tested sanguine/phlegmatic when he took the profile, and his wife, Keely, tested choleric/melancholy. Neither had characteristics of the other temperaments. This meant neither David nor Keely really understood the other's perceptions. In the early days of their marriage, this caused some frustration.

Had this not been the first marriage for either of them, and had they been a blended family, they probably would have brought into the marriage an underlying need to protect themselves and whatever children they had. The pain experienced in a previous marriage often keeps a person from giving a new mate the freedom to be himself or herself.

However, through the years, we have observed one predominant quality in David and Keely. Each has allowed the other to be himself or herself and they have not allowed the differences to control their relationship. Both of them are sincere in seeking to please God and we feel that is one of the main reasons for their successful marriage. God has blessed their relationship as they have worked with their differences.

Temperament Blends

God created each of us unique. We have mixes of characteristics that no one else has. How we display those traits are also original. Sometimes, our likes and dislikes may even seem to be in conflict and that may be confusing to others.

But we can discover some basic temperament combinations that will help explain why we act the way we do. This understanding will allow us to build smoother and more perceptive relationships with people of different personalities, and it will help us uncover our own hidden innate dispositions.

In your personality profile, you discovered primary and secondary temperaments. Let's look at how the two blend. Again, we'd like to credit Florence Littauer for sharing her insights into the personality types with us.

Some temperaments combine naturally because they have so many similar characteristics: for example, sanguine/choleric and melancholy/phlegmatic. These combinations are called **natural** blends. The sanguine/choleric is a leader who is optimistic, outgoing and outspoken. The melancholy/phlegmatic is analytical, pessimistic and soft-spoken.

Two of the temperament blends are **complementary**—they have some similar characteristics and some very different ones: sanguine/phlegmatic and choleric/melancholy. These combinations cause inner conflict in many people.

The sanguine/phlegmatic is the *play* combination. People with this blend are witty, easy-going and not goal oriented. They experience inner conflict, though, because their sanguine characteristics thrive on relationships, but the phlegmatic in them doesn't want to get involved.

Those who have this blend like to be alone, but then they find that isolation is not much fun. The sanguine in them wants to do something, but the phlegmatic wants to sit comfortably and regroup.

The choleric/melancholy is the *work* combination, intent on both doing a job and doing it perfectly. Those who have this blend are decisive, organized and goal oriented. Yet their different emotional levels (the choleric thinks tears are a sign of weakness, and the melancholy cries when he is happy, sad, angry or when he feels something deeply) and their need for people (the choleric needs people to accomplish a goal, and the melancholy needs people to care for him) cause friction within.

We call the other two combinations, sanguine/melancholy and choleric/phlegmatic, **opposite** blends. Their characteristics are so different that they have a hard time existing in the same person. When test results show either of these blends, that could be a signal that the person is wearing a mask.

Masking

What is masking? It's when you have taken on a temperament not natural to your personality for so long that you have forgotten who you really are. Masking can be caused by some real or imagined trauma or by misperceptions. Remember, your true temperaments are innate, so if you put on a mask, it will eventually want to come off.

When masking, unnatural characteristics are exhibited to an extreme. For instance, a person wearing a sanguine mask will not just be funny—he will act as the "class clown" or "fool." Someone with a choleric mask will try to control at all costs. The person in a melancholy mask will play the role of a victim or someone in pain and is usually deeply depressed. And someone under a phlegmatic mask will remove himself from any involvement with other people and appear to have no hope.

LaDean

Masking is prevalent in blended families, especially in children. For example, Trey first took the temperament profile when he was in junior high school. He tested sanguine/melancholy. I thought the test was correct. Trey is very outgoing, cute and funny, and he is intelligent and talented both musically and artistically.

As we began to learn more about temperaments, the Lord brought to my mind a few statements that Trey had made. Once I asked him, "Why do you always try to make people laugh?"

"Someone has to make this family happy," he replied emphatically.

At the time, I just smiled and nodded my head. My response confirmed his need to be a sanguine.

Another time, he asked, "Mom, why do you take me everywhere you go?"

"Because you are my sunshine, the bright spot in my day. You make me laugh." Again, I confirmed his need to be a sanguine—I had indicated I liked him that way.

But as Trey entered high school, I began to see how choleric he was. Gradually, I gave him verbal and implied permission to be his choleric self. At the end of his junior year, he was selected to be drum major in his senior year. He began to shine in his true temperament. The first time I saw him direct the band on the field, his leadership ability amazed me.

Since I have allowed him to be his true self, we sometimes compete for control, but both of us are happier expressing our true personalities. As a result, we can relax with each other, and his high school years have been a true joy.

When I first took the temperament test, I tested choleric/melancholy. Normally, this combination does not signal masking, but after going through the process of giving Trey freedom to be himself, I realized things in my life did not exactly jibe—I was wearing a mask, too.

I began to look for things I did that no one else saw. For example, the way I organized my closet was definitely sanguine. I took note of my filing cabinet. I had lots of pretty folders but loose organization.

The final clue was my baby pictures. I've heard it said that the eyes are the windows of the soul. My eyes sparkled sanguine. However, when I was three and my sister was born, I became serious and commanding.

Another indication of my true temperament came when I read Tim LaHaye's book, *Why People Act the Way They Do*. He described how each of the four temperaments drives a car. His description of a sanguine driver made me think he had been in my car with me. A sanguine driving down the road will talk with a passenger and look at his friend rather than at where he is going. When alone, the sanguine will drive fast, then slow down for no apparent reason, and then speed up again.

I couldn't believe it—this was me! So I began the process of removing layer after layer of my mask, much like peeling an onion. The effort has taken years.

If you are masking, you may need a professional (a pastor, counselor, etc.) to help you discover your true self. This can be frustrating, but it is also exciting. For instance, I used to know where all my possessions were, and now I can't find anything. I can't sit still for long periods of time as I once did. And I have also realized I can handle only so much seriousness before I must have some fun. But what a relief to act naturally!

I experienced these three steps in my process of change:

First, I became *aware* that a change was needed. I did this by taking the temperament profile and continuing a study of personality differences.

Second, I realized I had to *absorb* the change as it

happened. Give yourself time—it is a slow process. Sometimes we will take two steps forward and one backward, then two more forward and another backward. Don't let that discourage you. It is still progress.

And third, I had to *accept* that change is okay. And remember to give your loved ones time to adjust to your change. They may feel threatened because they are not sure we still love them or need them or even want them.

Don, too, struggled when he first discovered his temperaments. I'll let him tell his story.

Don

When I first took the personality profile, I tested sanguine/phlegmatic. This didn't necessarily indicate a mask. However, I didn't feel content and found myself seeking the real me.

Lana Bateman began the conscious process of helping me expose my innate self. I discovered a front-running choleric. That's why I achieved success as a football coach. On the field, I expressed my true self. Becoming what God created me to be gives me great joy. No wonder coaching brought me so much fulfillment.

Because I can discipline myself more easily now, I am winning some of the frustrating battles with my hardheadedness and overbearing attitude. I no longer feel I have to be right about everything or that I must force my viewpoint on everyone around me.

Looking in my closet or my files gives away my melancholy temperament. I wash, dry and iron my own shirts so they will be done correctly. I hang my clothes in the closet in groups so I can find each piece easily. My files are so organized that anyone could walk in and teach my students, though not as well as I, of course. I really am a creature of habit, but they are all perfect habits.

LaDean is gagging as she reads this, but how in the world can a sanguine understand proper organization?

We finally have discovered that Trey and I are both choleric/melancholy. LaDean is choleric/sanguine. We've got a lot of bosses in this house with no peacemaker!

Choosing Freedom

The only way we can live together is by choosing to give each other the freedom to be his own person. We taped a saying on our refrigerator door and on the bathroom mirror that sums up our position: "This relationship means too much to me to continue arguing over this." We committed ourselves to make our relationship count more than any circumstance.

We are not the same people we were. Now we are a lot happier and more at peace with ourselves and with each other than when we first married.

You, too, can find this same peace and happiness. We suggest a four-step process that will help smooth out personality traits between people who are both different and alike.

First, *pray for patience.* Before a disagreement explodes into a crisis, ask God what He desires for you in this matter. Then listen and heed His instructions.

Second, *postpone pessimism.* Take control of all words and actions that could be destructive.

Third, *pace power.* Any action should be taken under tight control. I have a poster in my room at school that says, "Nothing is stronger than gentleness, and nothing is more gentle than real strength." That advice has made the difference between a hot, angry reaction and a slower, gentler approach.

Fourth, *practice peace.* Seek peaceful solutions to the struggles that arise rather than try to figure out how to win.

In a blended family, differences are magnified. What you have learned about temperaments will give you a basis for understanding the conflict in your family. Perhaps for the first time you see the real reason for the struggles between yourself and those around you. Or maybe you are beginning to get a handle on why you and your partner always disagree over the same issues.

Remember that any change in your family begins with you. There are both advantages and disadvantages in being alike and being different. If you have married an opposite, you will experience conflict because of your two different viewpoints. However, you also have a great opportunity to use your strengths to complement what you perceive as weaknesses in your mate and to allow her strengths to help you with your weaknesses. Growth and understanding will result as you focus on similarities and give each other the freedom to be different.

MAKING OF A MIRACLE

Use your understanding of the temperament blends and masking as a foundation to begin the process of changing together.

As a couple, talk about the following questions. When you agree on the answers, write them down. Then share what you have written with your children.

1. Where are we in relation to our dreams and goals?

2. What is our vision?

3. What is our plan for achieving our vision?

4. Are we willing to commit our vision . . .
   . . . to the Lord?
   . . . to each other?
   . . . to hard work?

Blend for the week of _____

I can fool myself and the rest of the world for a
while but sometimes the real me will come forth.

For nothing is hidden, except to be revealed;
nor has anything been secret, but that it
should come to light.
(Mark 4:22, NAS)

Blessings for the week of _____

9

Two-Sided Coin

Don

It was football season, and my schedule was tight. We were to speak at Prestonwood Baptist Church in Dallas at 7 P.M., and I had to coach a game at 4.

We should win this game easily, I figured. *My players can run the ball to eat up the clock. I can leave right after the game. It's only a forty-five-minute drive. Plenty of time.*

I grabbed my suit, my boots, a dress shirt and tie, and I drove to the field which was near the freeway. After arriving, I discovered an earlier game was running late, so ours couldn't start until 4:45. When the clock ran out, I said goodbye to my team on the field and ran to my van. It was 6:40. Even rushing, I was already twenty-five minutes behind schedule!

Tearing down the freeway, I asked the Lord to make my path straight and free of smokeys. I decided I could save time by changing clothes in the van as I drove. I put the cruise control on seventy-five and began peeling off my coaching outfit. It took five miles to get my shirt and pants off.

As I flew through Irving, Texas, with only undershorts on, my boots and suit pants slid off the seat into the stepwell behind the passenger seat. I couldn't reach them. Glancing around, I grabbed my umbrella from the back, slid out of my seat and, steering with my left hand, stretched as far as I could with the umbrella handle to hook my clothes. I was going eighty by now. Checking the road out of the corner of my eye, I saw a patrolman on the shoulder of the freeway pointing his radar gun right at me. My heart jumped out of my throat. I was in my underwear, out of the driver's seat, going eighty! All I could think of was I had to get something on so I would not have to stand beside the road in my underwear.

I could hear LaDean: "You arrested him driving how fast? In his underwear?"

Jumping back into the driver's seat, I began madly pulling my coaching pants back on. "Help me, Lord," I pleaded. I started thinking, *What will I tell the officer if he stops me? That I'm on my way to speak at a Baptist church to a group of women attending a seminar entitled, "Women in Crisis"?*

Because God does answer the prayers of fools, the officer never moved. But I'm sure he had quite a story to tell back at the station.

I skidded into the church parking lot at exactly 7:10, fully dressed in my suit and tying my tie. *I'm late,* I worried. *LaDean will probably be speaking. Those women won't get to hear me.*

When I entered the auditorium, I discovered that the main session was behind schedule and, laughing, I sat down to catch my breath.

Suddenly, a sobering thought struck me. *I want the women to hear the material that LaDean and I prepared, but my main concern is that I'm supposed to be the one to give it. How absurd!*

What made my selfish attitude even more ridiculous was that LaDean had given the identical presentation earlier in the day.

Over the next few months, as I desired to learn something beyond the humor of this story, I began to realize that communication is more than a lot of talking. It was not enough for me to recognize my selfishness in the seminar situation. I needed to share with LaDean how this awareness had changed my attitude about our speaking and how it had given me real insight into being a meaningful communicator in our family. The instruction of the Lord in this matter took more than a year to begin to change me. Until then, our communication had been one-sided.

The Communication Cycle

Most married couples live together for years and never really communicate with each other. Our counselor, Brooke Annis, once told us, "You and LaDean remind me of a couple of parrots. You talk a lot, but you don't listen to each other."

Partners who don't express themselves clearly and listen carefully set up a destructive cycle that leads to misunderstanding and arguments. When a husband reacts indifferently to his wife, he affects how she feels about herself. In return, his reaction to her depends on her ability to express herself and on how well she listens. This cycle leads to contention and poor self-esteem.

Most of the fights LaDean and I had were over one or both of us saying, "You never listen to me!" We never shouted, "I never listen to you!"

As human beings, we are self-centered, and being heard is more important to us than hearing others. But communication is a two-sided coin: speaking *and* listening. There are many speech and writing classes at all levels of education to teach us to express ourselves effectively, but where are the listening classes? Some teachers and parents work hard at teaching listening skills, but many do not. This lack of listening skills shows up like neon lights in marriage communication. The Bible says in James 1:19: "But let everyone be quick to hear, slow to speak, and slow to anger" (NAS).

In the process of communication we cannot be only the speaker or only the listener, we are both. We each move in and out of these roles.

First, the speaker sends a message. How someone receives what we say is not our responsibility. We just have to say it.

Second, the listener receives what is said at face value. He does not make a judgment until he repeats what he thinks the speaker said.

Third, the speaker clarifies what he said using "I" messages to indicate that he accepts responsibility for his feelings. For example, "I feel sad when you do that"; or, "Yes, that is exactly what I meant"; or, "No, I really meant . . . "

Now the listener becomes the speaker as he responds to the clarification, and the speaker becomes the listener as he receives the results of his original message. This explanation seems rather lengthy, but the diagram shows how quickly the exchange happens:

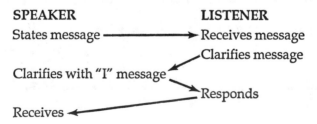

SPEAKER   **LISTENER**

States message ──────────▶ Receives message

Clarifies message

Clarifies with "I" message

Responds

Receives ◀

Although this communication cycle can prevent us from misinterpreting messages, we sometimes find ourselves falling into communication habits that distort the meaning of what we are hearing. A big part of the problem is that we don't pay attention to our partner.

Reflective Listening

In her Listening Skills Workshop, Brooke Annis introduced LaDean and me to a new concept: reflective listening. We have used this skill many times in our marriage, in our classrooms and in the workshops we teach. LaDean has applied this technique successfully in her life. She explains what reflective listening means and how to use it.

LaDean

Don loved the concept of reflective listening and applied it immediately to our relationship. I had difficulty adapting to the idea. It seemed silly to repeat what I had just heard. Because of my reluctance to use it, Don asked me to explain the concept in our workshops. He believed in the Mary Kay philosophy that you become stronger in any area that you teach.

Let's begin by describing what reflective listening does not do. It will not solve problems, give solutions or pass judgment. Now let that soak in for a minute. When I listen, I do not try to give the speaker my opinion, make assumptions about what I hear, or try to fix the speaker's problems.

Reflective listening is a mirror that merely reflects feelings or restates what you think the speaker has just said. The listener doesn't change the meaning or add his own interpretation. He waits for the speaker to clarify what he really feels or means.

Unfortunately, most of us have developed listening habits that are harmful to communication. These cartoons by Trey illustrate bad listening habits so perfectly that I want to share them with you. See if you recognize yourself.

Selective Listening

Insensitive Listening

Pseudo-Listening

Insulated Listening

Defensive Listening

Ambush Listening

Why is reflective listening different? What does it contribute to a conversation? It diffuses power struggles. It allows both the speaker and listener to control their emotions and communicate their feelings. It also gives the speaker an opportunity to hear what he said and to clarify his words and feelings.

Some of the phrases the listener could use include:

"If I understand what you mean, you're saying . . ."

"I think you mean . . ."

"Let me be sure I understand . . ."

"If I am hearing you correctly, you are feeling . . ."

Let me illustrate how effective reflective listening can be.

Five years ago, I taught a class of strong-willed cholerics. When an administrator came into my room to evaluate my teaching skills, the students decided to take control of the class discussion.

Immediately, I put my knowledge of temperaments and reflective listening into action. Because I knew cholerics like to buck authority, I decided to remove myself from a standing position which signified authority to the students. I asked them to put their chairs in a circle and I joined them. As the discussion continued, I used the phrases of reflective listening. This diffused the power struggle and allowed me to insert the information I wanted to give them.

Later, I overheard my appraiser telling another administrator, "She's the most persuasive teacher I've ever critiqued." Don and I use reflective listening in our home, too. He relates one such incident.

Don
―――――――――

One night during Trey's junior high years, LaDean cooked steak for supper.

"This meat's tough," Trey complained. "I can hardly chew it. And it's overcooked, too." He began to pout. "I don't really like steak anyway."

He was working hard to create a real conflict, and I calmly replied, "If I understand what you're saying, you feel the meat is too hard to chew, and you don't want to eat it."

His expression went blank, a typical "junior high jerk" look. Then he began to grin—his game was exposed. "Yes, that's right."

We left the situation right there for a few seconds. The conflict never happened, he ate the steak and our meal went on peacefully. Before learning about listening skills, I probably would have shouted, "You will eat that steak with your mouth or it will go in your ear!" LaDean likely would have come to his defense, and we'd be off!

I'm grateful that God is tempering my life through His power.

And how about that conflict we had over the Christmas tree lights so many years ago? Here's how we could have given that incident a happy ending.

When LaDean objected to the way David and I were putting on the lights, I could have replied, "If I am hearing you correctly, putting lights on the tree is a special time for you and Trey."

LaDean probably would have answered, "That's right. That's exactly how I feel."

Reflective listening would have let us get down to the real issue, that she felt something special to her and Trey was being taken away, rather than turning our conversation into an argument. We could have made our first Christmas a time to blend traditions and respect each other's feelings.

LaDean does not like for me to use reflective listening in our discussions, so it has become another way we use humor to help diffuse conflict. She will say, "Don't you use that on me!" but by this time we usually are already laughing.

Levels of Communication

Our lives, our workshops and our teaching have confirmed to us that effective communication is a major reason marriages are successful. This communication involves several levels of the big "I" word—intimacy. Intimacy is experienced in our feelings, so my level of intimate communication is determined by my willingness to express my feelings. Men seem to have more difficulty getting to the deeper levels of communication because they are more reluctant to reveal their true feelings.

The first level is *surface talk,* small talk such as, "How are you? Is everything all right?" or, "Sure is a beautiful day." We acknowledge the presence of the listener but little more. Still the door is opened for us to go on to the next level.

The second level is *newscasting.* Here we report happenings in the world or in our life. "Did you see the wreck on the freeway?" or, "I got all the errands completed I had to do today." This requires little or no feelings, but again the door is opened to proceed to the next level.

The third level is *window shopping.* We allow ourselves to experiment with expressing a few ideas and feelings to see how they are received, though retreat is still easy if we aren't comfortable. "I have a problem with how something was handled at the office today"; or, "I'm concerned about how we talk to each other." This level may seem scary because we must express feelings that may not be approved by the listener.

The fourth level is *opening the window.* Deeper communication takes place on this level because we are sharing our feelings and emotions. If we felt comfortable in the window shopping stage, we are now ready to reveal more of ourselves. We might say, "I'm feeling really good today about us and where we are going"; or, "I'm feeling angry about what is happening at the office." We are taking responsibility for our feelings and for the message we send.

The fifth level is *transparency*. Intimacy takes place here because you invite someone to see the real you with your fears and dreams. You risk rejection and realize that what you say can be used against you, but you have enough confidence in the relationship and in where God is taking it to open yourself up.

Communicators in this level usually have past experiences of shared feelings with each other which have created trust. One might say, "Honey, my greatest fear is that you will leave me. Sometimes that fear terrifies me." Or, "I have trauma in my past that I must deal with. I want you to be with me as I relive and grow through this."

Transparency is the door to intimacy. It must be nurtured. If I use my partner's trust against her, that will drive her away from me with a new wound. But couples who learn to communicate sensitively will bond more completely.

Nonverbal Messages

Communication includes not only verbal but also nonverbal messages. Remember the body language discussion regarding the temperaments? Tone of voice and body language give emotion to verbal communication. The amount of the total communication cycle process you use allows you and your mate to achieve whatever level of communication you feel comfortable with. There should be no guilt associated with the two of you choosing your preferred level.

If at any point in working through the levels of communication you fail to use listening skills, the right tone of voice or the correct body language to support your words, you could shut the whole thing down. As you desire to move to a deeper level, ask for the Lord's help.

Be sensitive about where God is taking you and where your mate is in your communication level. Don and I have found we move in and out of some of the levels. One of the neat things about understanding these levels of communication and having Christ as our Lord is that we can be on any level and still please Him.

To build communication in your marriage, ask the Lord also to help you control your words and become an effective listener. Practice both sides of the communication coin to help strengthen your bond and build your mate's self-esteem. Control your speech to protect your intimacy and closeness. These skills will lead you further on your journey to marital wholeness and harmony.

To help you begin the process, we have included some questions that measure how much you know about each other. Ask yourself the questions and record the answers. Have your spouse do the same. Then compare results. Discussing your responses will open doors to intimacy through communication.

This openness can be best accomplished if you mutually agree to respect each other's confidences and to avoid using answers against each other in the future. Deep sharing requires careful safeguards to protect each other's vulnerability.

1. What does your partner value, both in life and in a mate?

2. What does he/she fear most, both in life and in a marriage?

3. Which experience does he/she consider the best in his/her life? The most difficult?

4. What are his/her goals?

5. If he/she could change anything about me, what would it be?

6. What does he/she like best about me?

7. What could I do to enhance his/her self-image?

As you discuss what each values, has experienced, and wants to do with his or her life, you will have an opportunity to share your answers to these same questions concerning your life. Talking over your responses at the same time will help both of you feel more comfortable about confessing shortcomings. And you will gain valuable insights into your partner's dreams and hopes.

MAKING OF A MIRACLE

In our workshops, we use situation exercises to practice these skills. We divide into groups of two, not husbands and wives, but males and females. (We do this to prevent arguments in the middle of the workshop.) This exercise will work just as effectively with your family. One person is the designated speaker and the other is the listener. The speaker selects the subject, something that has happened recently, and the listener reflects. After working through the communication cycle, the partners switch roles and work through the cycle again.

It takes time to absorb this concept and effort to make it work. We must concentrate in order to be good listeners. As we learn to listen effectively, the whole message will be more clear to us.

An alternative to reflective listening is the use of a referee. At one point in our marriage we had to take turns being the referee, a week at a time. The referee can call time-out at any point in a discussion and both parties must cease talking. During the time-out we would write down what we were feeling. Then we would come back together to discuss what we had written.

We urge you to practice these skills in your home with as many family members as possible.

Blend for the week of _____

All can hear, but only the sensitive can understand.

He who gives an answer before he hears,
it is folly and shame to him.
(Proverbs 18:13, NAS)

Blessings for the week of _____

10

Manning the Battleship

Don

On December 6, 1863, the Confederate navy vessel *Weehawken* lay peacefully anchored off the port of Charleston. Part of a new class of battleships called monitors, it was ironclad and equipped with heavy guns fitted into a revolving turret. In battle, it could cause extensive damage to older, wooden ships.

Since ventilation wasn't good inside, the crew opened her forehatch. Meanwhile, a mild gale began whipping up heavy swells. As the ship rocked with the waves, her cable and anchor wells filled with sea water. No one on board noticed.

Soon, the front part of the ship began dipping lower, and rolling waves poured through the bulkhead doors. By the time an alert was sounded, the *Weehawken* could not be saved. She sank while "safe" in port.

Many of us live our Christian lives unmindful of the dangers we face. We came to know the Lord as God intended, in a setting of love and gentleness, and we quickly began to enjoy the peace and security of being part of God's family. Suddenly, waves of temptation and sin engulf us. Do we know how to respond?

Christ did not call us to relax on a pleasure ship; He called us to serve on a battleship. We cannot afford to lay back in the midst of the forces arrayed against us—the pull of the world, the wiles and might of Satan and his kingdom, and the battle against temptation within oneself.

Do you sometimes feel like you are losing the spiritual battle in your household? Or fear for a family member entangled in sin? Many couples find themselves floundering over how to combat the forces of evil.

But God has assured us victory through His Son, Jesus Christ, who said, "In the world you will have tribulation, but take courage; I have overcome the world" (John 16:33, NAS).

The apostle John writes:

> Whatever is born of God overcomes the world; and this is the victory that has overcome the world—our faith. And who is the one who overcomes the world, but he who believes that Jesus is the Son of God? (1 John 5:4,5, NAS)

Many books are written and sermons are preached on spiritual warfare. They deal with God versus Satan in heaven and in the garden of Eden, Christ on the cross, and the coming Battle of Armageddon.

However, we are going to look at the personal battle within yourself and the steps you can take to victory. We also will include the effect of the battle on your family and how you can go to war for your family members.

Our own spiritual battle starts the moment we join God's family. His Holy Spirit indwells us and begins to work Christ's holiness within us, but at the same time our old self, the sin nature, seeks to continue to control us. This conflict is called *spiritual warfare*. We will examine this battle in five steps: definition, weapons, consecration, execution and victorious salvation.

Before we go any further, however, we urge you to prepare yourself to study this subject. Ask God to open your heart to His truth. Place your Bible near by. Don't accept anything we say as etched in stone, but test any new information against the Word of God and the Lord's instructions to you. Give Him the freedom to change your heart and mind.

1. Definition

Spiritual warfare is the daily battle I wage within myself in the power of the Holy Spirit to bring my human nature (my flesh) under the control of a Christ-like spirit. My conflict is not with the "troubles" in my life but with the "struggle" to seek holiness within those troubles. The trials are merely the battleground God uses to bring me to Himself.

This warfare rages continuously. The Bible tells us: "For the flesh sets its desire against the Spirit, and the Spirit against the flesh; for these are in opposition to one another" (Galatians 5:17, NAS).

Where does this battle originate? James identifies the source; he says that the battle is within ourselves: "What is the source of quarrels and conflicts among you? Is not the source your pleasures that wage war in your members?" (James 4:1, NAS)

Peter explains: "Abstain from fleshly lusts, which wage war against the soul" (1 Peter 2:11, NAS).

Spiritual warfare begins in my thought life when my own evil desires are tempted to enjoy the world's lusts and attractions or are enticed by Satan's wiles. Therefore, my struggle is not with my spouse nor my children, but with the conflict going on inside my own mind and spirit. Understanding the source frees me to direct my efforts to the heart of the battle.

2. Weapons

Imagine yourself as a soldier facing a huge battle against a well-equipped enemy. What would your first concern be? Having your defenses and weapons in order.

God warns us that we face formidable spiritual foes: "Our struggle is not against flesh and blood, but against rulers . . . against the spiritual forces of wickedness in the heavenly places" (Ephesians 6:12, NAS).

Since we are in a spiritual battle, our weapons are spiritual in nature:

> For though we walk in the flesh, we do not war according to the flesh, for the weapons of our warfare are not of the flesh, but divinely powerful for the destruction of fortresses. We are destroying speculations and every lofty thing raised up against the knowledge of God, and we are taking every thought captive to the obedience of Christ (2 Corinthians 10:3-5, NAS).

God throws all the power of heaven into any battle I engage in for His glory and provides divine weapons beyond any strength I might muster on my own. Let's look at each of the weapons described in Ephesians chapter 6:

> Stand firm therefore, having *girded your loins with truth,* and having put on the *breastplate of righteousness* (verse 14, NAS).

When I gird myself with truth, I believe God is God and that He has done what His Word says He has done. Knowing God's will and His commands protects my spiritual vital organs from evil and prevents Satan from leading me into his lies and half-truths.

The breastplate of righteousness refers to the holiness which Christ has given me. This holiness gives me confidence and courage for the battle and protects my heart and other vulnerable areas from sin's destroying powers.

And having shod your feet with the *preparation of the gospel of peace* (verse 15, NAS).

Strong military boots protect a soldier's feet and allow him to march surely over rugged terrain. Gospel preparation—Bible study, Scripture memorization and meditation—shields my idle time from sin, and inner peace gives me purpose in sharing Christ's "good news" with others.

In addition to all, taking up the *shield of faith* with which you will be able to extinguish all the flaming missiles of the evil one (verse 16, NAS).

Faith is believing in something I cannot see. My trust in God's wisdom and power shields me from sin's lure, causing Satan's deadly attacks to fall harmlessly at my feet.

And take the *helmet of salvation*, and the *sword of the Spirit*, which is the word of God (verse 17, NAS).

A soldier's gleaming, metal headgear protects his most vital organ, the brain. Satan desires to control our minds. But the salvation of Jesus gives us a new heart with renewed thought processes and desires which help defend us from evil desires and pride.

The Word of God is a powerful weapon that we can use to repel false doctrine and teaching. The more I know of God and His Word, the more easily I can see and avoid the evil in the world. When we firmly grasp our sword and wield it in the power of the Holy Spirit, we avail ourselves of God's priceless wisdom in how to resist temptation.

3. Consecration

Consecration means giving God permission to

cleanse us and make us more like Him. But God will not violate my will. If I won't submit myself to Him, I will have to fight my battles without His power.

On the other hand, allowing God to plow my heart and purge my thoughts and desires lets me view things from His perspective. My family sees God at work in me which becomes a powerful force to teach them to trust Him also.

Consecration gives parents the opportunity to represent Christ in their home. As husbands, we can function as priests to our household. When a father is not present, Mom fills that role and God's power will be just as strong. Job provides a godly example:

> Job would send and consecrate [his sons], rising up early in the morning and offering burnt offerings according to the number of them all; for Job said, "Perhaps my sons have sinned and cursed God in their hearts." Thus Job did continually (Job 1:5, NAS).

As a priest, I have the great honor of "standing in the gap" for my family. Intercession is an intense prayer for someone in which I allow God to lay some of the pressure this person is facing on me. This is what victorious parenting is all about. Instead of complaining, I seek God's will in me to deal with the weakness and sin in my family. If I feel myself or another family member under the attack of Satan, I use the phrase, "I bind you, Satan, out of our thoughts and our lives in the name of Jesus." Exercising God's power brings great conquest.

Because of my misspent youth, I pray daily that my sons will resist lustful sins. I bind and cast off Satan's efforts to destroy their purity. It is not my job to make sure they live "right"; it is God's business. But I can take comfort in His promise not to lose any that are His (John 17:12).

I also have the privilege of sharing God's Word with my family. This is a great gift and an awesome responsibility. Through my own devotional time and family Bible reading, my wife and children see my commitment to God's Word and my dedication to allowing His Spirit to work out His principles in my daily life.

4. Execution

Now that I have consecrated myself, I begin to cleanse my own house. Through prayer, and sometimes fasting, LaDean and I dedicate all that we have to God as an expression of our inward commitment to Him.

We do this with any car we buy and also with our home. We dedicate every room, the yard and the driveway. My sons were given to God on their eighteenth birthdays, and we celebrated a special time with Trey when he turned eighteen. Our purpose is to keep in mind God's ownership of all He has entrusted to us, including our children.

5. Victorious Salvation

The same divine power that destroys evil saves those who are redeemed of God. Philippians 1:27,28 assures us:

> You are standing firm in one spirit, with one mind striving together for the faith of the gospel; in no way alarmed by your opponents—which is a sign of destruction for them, but of salvation for you, and that too, from God (NAS).

What a promise! I experience victory when I depend on His power and trust Him to fulfill His promises.

We urge you to take three steps to complete the process of victory.

First, *decide to be a warrior of the cross.* This includes accepting Jesus Christ as your Savior and also making Him Lord of your life.

Second, *join a group of warriors.* Don't expect perfection from your co-laborers in Christ. Look for Christians who are struggling but who have joined the battle. A group like this will support and love you.

Third, *put your life on the line.* Fight for your family. Dedicate yourself to allowing God to do His mighty work in you.

No victory is won without a battle. Although you may feel discouraged at times by the power of the forces attacking you, keep fighting. God has promised to contend for you: "For the LORD your God is the one who goes with you, to fight for you against your enemies, to save you" (Deuteronomy 20:4, NAS).

Ask the Holy Spirit to fill you with His power and might for the big—and for the little—skirmishes you face.

MAKING OF A MIRACLE

Our Blend Card for this chapter has a positive statement regarding our attitude toward struggle. We pray for each of you that you will not be afraid of change as you prepare your battleship for war. It is sometimes difficult, but the results are always positive as we journey toward harmony.

Make sure you put this card on your key ring as a reminder to read the verse daily.

At this point your Blessing Cards may be getting good stroking remarks. Look for God's grace in all situations.

Blend for the week of _____

I see life's challenges not as stumbling blocks, but as building blocks.

> *For our struggle is not against flesh and blood,*
> *but against the rulers . . . powers . . . world forces*
> *of this darkness . . . [and] spiritual forces*
> *of wickedness in the heavenly places.*
> (Ephesians 6:12, NAS)

Blessings for the week of _____

11

Wise Battle Plans

Don

The king of Syria plotted to destroy the nation of Israel. He mobilized his forces and marched to a certain place to ambush the Israelite army.

But the prophet Elisha warned the Israelite king of the trap, and the enemy's scheme was thwarted.

After this had happened several times, the Syrian king sent a scout to see why the Hebrew army always knew about his plans. The scout returned to say, "Elisha, the prophet, tells the king of Israel even the words you speak in the privacy of your bedroom!" (2 Kings 6:12, TLB)

So one night, Syrian forces surrounded the city in which Elisha was living. The next morning, Elisha's servant discovered chariots, troops and horses besieging them. He ran inside and informed the prophet. The servant cried despairingly, "Alas, my master, what shall we do now?"

"Don't be afraid!" Elisha said. "For our army is bigger than theirs!" (2 Kings 6:15,16, TLB)

He prayed, and the young servant's eyes were opened. He saw horses and chariots of fire surrounding the Syrian army. Supernatural forces were protecting the city!

When the Syrian army attacked, Elisha asked the Lord to blind the soldiers' eyes. Then he led the sightless enemy troops to his own capital, right into the hands of the Israelite forces.

As blended partners, we, too, need special vision to battle the unique problems in our homes. The Lord will give us the strength and insight to build peace. James 1:5 says, "If any of you lacks wisdom, let him ask of God, who gives to all men generously and without reproach, and it will be given to him" (NAS).

Family life built upon the foundation of God's wisdom will be rich and full. Proverbs says: "By wisdom a house is built, and by understanding it is established; and by knowledge the rooms are filled with all precious and pleasant riches" (24:3,4, NIV).

Just as Elisha called upon the Lord to show his servant God's battle plans, so we can ask Him to guide us in facing the special conflicts in our lives.

LaDean and I have discovered several ways to avoid dangerous situations and turn them into circumstances that can build intimacy. We want to share practical suggestions to help you recognize and handle danger zones in family living. First, we encourage husbands to listen to their wives.

Listening to Each Other

LaDean seems to have a direct pipeline to God's will in some situations. When we began our ministry to families, we did several seminars for free. Then we began to feel "experienced," and we started considering how much we should charge for our workshops.

Some of our conferees were enthusiastic:

> "When I attended your seminar, I felt there was no alternative for my marriage except divorce. Thank

you for helping me see that I'm not the only one feeling this way. I now have hope."

"Your instruction has improved my marriage. Thank you!"

"This seminar would be a blessing to any church."

My vision quickly went from a national focus to a universal one. I began to get big-headed about the monetary value of our ministry.

"This is God's work," LaDean reminded me. "Let's ask Him how much we should charge."

After we prayed, I still had big numbers in mind, both people and money.

LaDean countered, "We need to tend the flock God has given us, no matter how small. Let's not think too big."

I wasn't listening—to her or to God.

One day, a big church called to schedule a conference. I was ecstatic. Naturally, my estimate of our ministry was more accurate than LaDean's.

But no one came to the seminar. Not even one person.

Shortly after, we visited another pastor. He was blunt: "You are asking too much money."

LaDean didn't say, "I told you so," but the Lord had spoken loud and clear. He had been trying to get my attention through my wife, but I had not listened.

I urge you husbands to be especially sensitive to your wives in spiritual warfare. When she brings you a word of concern, give heed. The sweet, gentle spirit God has given wives often responds to spiritual matters more quickly than our spirit does.

Hedge of Thorns

Some of our greatest spiritual warfare will be for

family members in need. We practice making loving intercession for that person by praying a hedge of thorns around him.

In Old Testament times, hedges were thick, woven fences of bushes with sharp thorns facing outward formed into a circle like a corral. They kept sheep in and predators out.

We believe the Bible gives two kinds of prayers to erect a hedge around our loved ones. The first one shields from harm and repels the enemy.

In Job 1:10 Satan accuses God of erecting a hedge of thorns around Job and his loved ones: "Hast Thou not made a hedge about him and his house and all that he has, on every side?" (NAS) We can ask God for the same protection from evil for our family. That doesn't mean we get in the way of God's work in a family member's life, only that we desire to shield our loved one from sin and Satan's evil plans.

Many divorced spouses pray for this hedge of thorns each time their child visits an absent parent. Often, an absent mother or father prays a hedge around the child because of the frightening living conditions that child is in every day. God is trustworthy and willing to care for any child.

The second kind of hedge is what we call a saving hedge. We pray this hedge when we feel the loved one must be allowed to suffer the consequences of their choices. Some describe it as tough love. Hosea 2:6,7 says:

> I will hedge up her way with thorns, and I will build a wall against her so that she cannot find her paths. And she will pursue her lovers, but she will not overtake them; and she will seek them, but will not find them. Then she will say, "I will go back to my first husband, for it was better for me then than now" (NAS).

Although this passage refers to a wayward wife, we apply the principle to anyone who strays from God's will.

We ask the Lord to erect a thorny hedge around the unrepentant one, to make him as uncomfortable as possible inside in order to bring him back into relationship with God. We ask Him to make our loved one's corrupt decision like vomit in his mouth and sickness in his belly. This may sound harsh, but it is consecrated tough love.

I prayed for a saving hedge for my son, Paul.

After LaDean and I married, both my sons had a tough time adjusting to Dad's new life. Paul was living in Texas and worked at a large rock-and-roll club. He lived in dangerous and evil surroundings, and at one point had been shot at.

One night, I lay awake worried about him. For months he hadn't returned my telephone calls. Finally, I got up and dressed. I gently shook LaDean. "I'm going to Dallas to talk to Paul. If I'm not home by 2 A.M., call my brother Jim."

I got to the club and finally found Paul. He and I sat on a stairway and talked for about fifteen minutes.

"I love you so much, Paul," I began, my heart aching. "You belong to the Lord. I pray for you every day. Please remember that."

I wept and prayed all the way home. Forcing back the tears, I told LaDean, "I don't think I got through to him. I'm really scared that one of these days we'll get a call telling us that Paul is either seriously hurt or dead."

Bowing my head, I prayed, "Oh, Lord, You know how my heart aches for my son. He is living so far from You. Please put a hedge around him." A vivid picture of the saving hedge protecting my son stuck in my mind. I paused, tears choking my words. "Lord, this is so hard for me to say. But if it is Your will, if there is nothing else anyone can do, and he strays too far, take him home to be with You. If necessary, You can even take my life if it will bring him back to you." I put my arms around LaDean.

A couple of months later, Paul brought a girl he was dating to our Christmas celebration. I was delighted to see him.

Before he left, the two of them came to me.

To my joy, Paul said, "I've quit my job at the club."

His girlfriend nodded. "I was so frightened for him. I told him I would quit seeing him unless he got out of that place."

I took her hand. "I don't know what the future holds for you and Paul, but I'll be grateful to you forever for caring so much for my son. You're an answer to my prayers."

To our delight, Paul's relationship with the Lord is being restored.

These hedges are gifts from God to help us pray for our families. Don't ask for an easy life. Instead, pray that the Lord will rescue you and your family from sin. Allow Him to perform His will in His way and timing to help you grow strong in Christ.

Trash Can Circumstances

Wars are fought on battlegrounds. Since our conflict begins within ourselves, we can identify certain areas that signal conflict. We call these battlefields "Trash Can Circumstances" because they belong in the trash can. They include anger, abusiveness, fear, jealousy, lust, pride, a sharp tongue and worldliness. We can get out of their grasp by asking God to help us throw them out of our lives. Then the only way they can escape after we put them in the trash can is if we remove the lid and let them out.

God never throws away anything unholy without replacing it with His holiness. Each of these Trash Can Circumstances has an opposite quality that God wants to build into us. As we accept this replacement, our lives will radiate with the nature of Christ.

One of the most prevalent Trash Can Circumstances in blended families is anger. Because LaDean had to deal with this conflict in her life, she explains how to have victory.

LaDean

1. Anger

Anyone who has ever lived with an angry person knows how fast an innocent situation can become unmanageable. That is frightening for those experiencing the effects and for the person who is out of control. As parents, we often do not teach our children how to handle their anger. This affects their future relationships, and it robs our family of the joy that God wants to give. God wants to replace anger with His joy, an inner happiness that does not depend on circumstances.

One day, Don and I heard a sermon by Charles Clary, pastor of Tate Springs Baptist Church in Arlington, Texas. He explained that anger has five levels. It begins with *irritation* or being bothered by something, and progresses to *indignation*, realizing that a wrong has been done. Next comes *wrath*, which results in reactions such as throwing something or kicking the dog. The next level is *fury* which is brutal and vengeful. You begin to feel "beside yourself," which may lead to violence. The final stage is *rage*. Now you have totally lost control and may not even remember the violent things you have done.

Pastor Clary's explanation made me begin some heavy duty praying and soul searching. It took me a long time to realize I had been angry for years. Sometimes I was not aware of why I felt angry or at whom. But the feeling went with me everywhere, and it surfaced every now and then. In fact, when I felt the happiest, I would subconsciously find something that irritated me so I could express my hostility.

My anger seemed to stay in the irritation and indignation stages, but sometimes it progressed to wrath. How many times had I slammed cabinet doors when someone crossed me?

Suddenly, I realized, *the Lord has choreographed my steps.* First, He had led me to hear a sermon on controlling anger, then to a godly counselor who helped create an inner peace in me, and finally to discover the temperaments.

The Lord began to replace my anger with joy, and I began to feel a peace beyond my understanding. Now when I am irritated, my responses are much calmer. When you have inner peace, even the anger you sometimes feel is filtered through the peace. But when your inner being is filled with anger, everything is filtered through that anger and there is no peace.

We also have found that modeling godly responses and teaching our children how to turn their resentments and outrage over to the Lord (instead of hanging on to them) produce joy in their lives and in the family. Perhaps this would be the perfect time to recall: "Be angry, and yet do not sin; do not let the sun go down on your anger" (Ephesians 4:26, NAS).

2. Abusiveness

Abuse can be physical, emotional or spiritual. Whether someone has mistreated you or you have misused a loved one, God can replace that circumstance with mercy. Focus on how much mercy He has given you so you can freely give mercy to others.

3. Fear

Fear is from Satan. He would love to see us cower with worry because he realizes we will never find victory when anxiety controls our lives. God replaces fear with cheerfulness. Paul writes: "You have not received a spirit of slavery leading to fear again, but you have received a spirit of adoption as sons by which we cry out, 'Abba! Father!'" (Romans 8:15, NAS) This cheerfulness is not a Pollyanna optimism that everything will turn out fine, but a confidence in what our loving heavenly Father is doing in our lives.

4. Jealousy

Old green-eyed jealousy thrives in a family where hurtful pasts continue to haunt. The Bible describes the results: "Where jealousy and selfish ambition exist, there is disorder and every evil thing" (James 3:16, NAS).

God replaces jealousy with trust, the foundation stone of loving with freedom. If you find yourself struggling with suspicion, ask the Lord to build trust in your relationship. Hand over to your heavenly Father all those past experiences that hinder your ability to believe in your mate. Let Him have the burden of helping your partner maintain his love for you.

5. Lust

Almost everyone battles lust at some time. But wrongful cravings can be replaced with a godly attitude toward sex. It is God's gift for marriage delight.

Nurturing your sexual relationship will build intimacy which will thwart evil desires. Thank the Lord daily for the mate He has given you. Appreciate your partner's lovely and alluring ways and take time for cozy moments and relaxing play.

6. Pride

Pride is simply self-love. The Book of Proverbs gives us severe warnings against this sin: "When pride comes, then comes dishonor" (11:2, NAS). "Pride goes before destruction, and a haughty spirit before stumbling"

(16:18, NAS). "An arrogant man stirs up strife" (28:25, NAS).

God overshadows pride with helpfulness. When we focus on helping others, we become givers instead of takers. Our selfish desires are changed and channeled into giving to others.

7. A Sharp Tongue

If you battle tongue control, you understand how words can devastate. James 3:5 explains, "The tongue is a small part of the body, and yet it boasts of great things. Behold, how great a forest is set aflame by such a small fire!" (NAS)

God wants to teach us to control our tongues by speaking kindness. Ask Him to help you think before you open your mouth. Be quick to compliment or reinforce the good things you see in others and look for ways to build up your partner or your children in tense situations.

8. Worldliness

I once heard the saying, "We do all right as long as we love people and use things. But we immediately cause problems when we love things and use people." God created this world and the things in it for our enjoyment.

But our Lord redeemed us to prepare us for His kingdom in heaven, not to live permanently on this earth accumulating material wealth. To maintain a godly perspective, keep in mind that everything here is temporal and to be used for God's glory.

Whenever you find yourself dragging one of these eight attitudes out of the trash can, confess your sin to the Lord. Remember where these Trash Can Circumstances originate and what they can lead to, and immediately put the lid on them.

Spiritual warfare is truly a "Danger Zone" in blended families. We will travel through its battleground our entire lives. But we have victory when we live in God's power and fight like strong, courageous warriors. Our family grows and bonds in an atmosphere of godliness and success. Peace and joy fills our relationships. And we lessen discord and disharmony.

MAKING OF A MIRACLE

We encourage you to use a Bible concordance and look up every reference to human anger. Make a list of practical methods of controlling yourself.

Set a time with your mate to enjoy cozy moments and relaxing play.

Extend mercy to someone in your family who has wronged you.

Trust God to put a hedge around a family member.

Blend for the week of _____

In one of his speeches, former President Ronald Reagan said, "Through the pain, our hearts have been opened to a profound truth—the future is not free; the story of all human progress is one of a struggle against all odds."

For the weapons of our warfare are not of the flesh but divinely powerful for the destruction of fortresses.
(2 Corinthians 10:4, NAS)

Blessings for the week of _____

12

The Money Crunch

Don

When we got married in early December, the state of my finances shocked LaDean. She began to realize our desperate situation on the last leg of our honeymoon.

Forty miles from home we realized we were starving. LaDean said, "I sure would like a big, fat, juicy cheeseburger. How much money do we have left?"

I counted my change. "I have three dollars."

She stared at the coins. "I knew we were broke, but I didn't think it was this bad." The she counted her change and came up with two dollars. "Well, we can't eat on five dollars," she said disgustedly.

I said, "Yes we can, if we share."

So we did stop to eat. We bought one burger, two drinks and one order of fries. And we shared.

Things didn't get much better financially when we got home. For months, the only entertainment we could afford was the dollar movie. We were thankful for the dollar movie because it was our only entertainment except each other, and at that point we were not very entertaining.

Few issues are more emotional than the issue of finances. Since it is so emotional, many couples in a second marriage—for fear of destroying the relationship—do not discuss budgets, wills, estate plans, life insurance, college expenses or distribution of assets and liabilities. They don't want to bring them up, not because they don't understand the need to talk about them, but because there are so many variables and the issues are so complex. There are no absolute right or wrong answers, and there aren't many sources of guidance.

Yet handling finances and setting monetary policies is essential, especially in blended marriages. Avoiding budgets and schedules only leads to worse entanglements and liabilities. Misunderstandings over what is whose and what we should do with our assets can spark bitter disagreements. Our pastor gave us wise advice when he told us during a counseling session, "Unless you are willing to commit your finances to each other, you are not willing to commit your lives to each other."

Of course, the first step for anyone toward financial health is to commit everything you own to the Lord Jesus. The psalmist writes: "The earth is the LORD's and all it contains, the world, and those who dwell in it" (Psalm 24:1, NAS).

You don't really own your possessions. You are stewards, or managers, of what God has given you, and He holds you accountable. We firmly believe this, but at the same time we recognize that the complications of blended family living prevent it from being quite this simple.

As you work at planning your financial future together, we would like you to be aware of these three distinctive areas unique to blended families: conditions, obligations and expectations.

1. Financial Conditions

When a man and a woman begin a blended marriage, often their financial state is not equal. Although a divorce causes a money crunch for both parties, statistics show that most men improve their standard of living while most women reduce theirs. Often, one of the marriage partners suffers from a financial slump or poor planning.

The idea that two people can live as cheaply as one is a myth, particularly in blended marriages. If one party is in financial straits, that can color his decision to marry, especially if the other person has assets such as a house, savings accounts, trusts, inheritances or family wealth. These same "advantages" can also cause dissension later.

Although LaDean and I did not marry for money, our financial conditions were quite different from each other when we were newlyweds. My checkbook and credit were a mess. She had saved and spent carefully. For the first five years of our marriage, we struggled to make ends meet because of the indebtedness that I had incurred. That put extra stress on our relationship. I am grateful that God gave LaDean patience to help straighten out my finances.

Whether you are planning to marry, are newlyweds or have been partners for years, we urge you to carefully evaluate your financial condition. Until you know the real picture, you cannot begin to rectify the problems and plan for the future.

2. Financial Obligations

Obligations brought into a blended marriage are often numerous and long-term. Child-support payments, indebtedness from the previous marriage, joint property ownership with an ex-spouse, educational and medical responsibilities, and a desire to provide allowances and cars for children can make family finances complicated and stressful.

These obligations resemble waves on a beach. At times they trickle in, other times they roll in and sometimes they crash in. Correctly responding to the ebb and flow can keep us from being carried out to sea.

Wise partners float with their changing situation. They deal immediately with any resentment over a mate's attention to an ex-spouse's financial problems or frustration over a generous divorce decree or pre-nuptial agreement. Sometimes you have to "go with the flow" in unforeseen situations.

For example, one single parent with a teenage son suddenly lost her job and was without work for several months. Her ex-husband, who was remarried, provided extra money until she found employment. His current wife had difficulty accepting his generosity. Her reaction could either damage their marriage relationship or help her husband manage in a difficult circumstance. She wisely helped stretch finances to better cope with the reduced budget.

How would you respond in a similar situation? Many spouses try to hide these kinds of financial decisions from their mate. But secrecy like this is poison to a marital relationship.

Remember, blood runs thicker than water. Objecting to the handling of a crisis will only impair the love between you and your mate.

Sometimes we also allow our children to jeopardize our relationship. A west Texas friend in a second marriage had her new husband's children, both non-working high school graduates, move in with them. The sudden demands on their budget increased the level of frustration in their home. The couple began having tremendous difficulty communicating. LaDean and I pray that the parents will learn to ebb and flow with the new pressures and that they will seek professional help.

Often couples who hurt in one area of their relationship will try to bring attention to the pain by disagreeing in another area. Financial concerns are especially vulnerable to this temptation. Sometimes a man and wife will not share sexually when the real problem is stress over finances. Or a couple may use money issues to punish each other for disagreements over household duties.

To avoid using finances as a battleground, discuss your obligations at a time when you can talk calmly and logically. Being honest about the financial stresses you face will help you avoid sheltering these difficulties behind another area in your relationship.

3. Financial Expectations

When John and Carrie married, she expected him to provide the same standard of living she had enjoyed in her previous marriage. But John had extensive monthly payments for a new business he had started several years before and also helped to support his three children who lived with his ex-wife.

One day soon after the wedding, Carrie announced, "We need new living room furniture. I'd like to redecorate."

John stared at her in disbelief. "What are you talking about? You know very well we can't afford anything like that."

Carrie's face hardened. "We have enough in our savings account."

"Not a chance. I have income taxes coming up. I'll need every penny." He raised the newspaper and refused to discuss the subject any further.

Neither John nor Carrie spoke to each other for three days. And even after they made up, their disagreement smoldered under the surface.

Expectations in a blended marriage are often magnified because one spouse brings more assets into the marriage than the other and retains the desire to control those premarital assets. With higher levels of obligations, balancing checkbooks and budgets can be hazardous to bonding. And the process of setting financial priorities can be heart-wrenching.

When we marry for the second time, we think we are wiser, but we often still have a fairy-tale idea of marriage. Because we have an established career, a home and a bank account, we believe life will be easier this time. We set high goals for ourselves.

Not only that, but we also may think setting up a budget is a logical, simple process. Then suddenly we find that our already established and different ways of handling finances conflict with each other. To make matters worse, the money crisis you never expected crops up.

How do you handle such touchy situations? Does it work to forgive and forget? What happens if you still don't agree after discussing every possibility and compromise? Will these issues cause permanent division between you and your loved ones?

The Middle Man

Blended families have such unique financial challenges that couples sometimes need a mediator to help them untangle the mess. This could be a counselor, a financial consultant or a respected minister. Although adding a third party takes some of the romance out of the relationship, finances are the business part of the marriage and should be handled in a business-like manner. Seek out a godly man or woman who cannot only help you plan wisely but who also knows the principles of stewardship found in the Bible.

We also recommend a middle man in making a will. This is a touchy area for most blended couples. We found that when things were going well between us, we didn't want to spoil the mood of the moment. And we certainly weren't going to discuss such delicate issues when we were angry. We also wondered if our relationship was secure enough to withstand the strain of deciding such complex financial matters. So we put off writing a will for several years.

When we finally sat down to make our will, we faced many hard decisions. LaDean has one son and I have two. How do we divide our estate? Do we split it in half, with her son getting half and my sons getting the other half? Or do we divide everything into thirds?

How do we itemize and distribute what we had before our marriage? And what we have acquired since then? What about investments and possessions that are a mixture of before and after such as the house we bought together?

There are no rules for fairness, even in the courts. We discovered no "right" or "wrong" answers. That makes it hard to arrive at equitable solutions. But we did realize that this task must be handled with love, tolerance and fairness.

That's why we believe it is important for a blended family to seek out an attorney who is familiar with the unique financial problems in blended families. Ask him to coordinate your accumulated properties with a comprehensive estate plan. You may need to schedule two visits, one to exchange information and the other to examine suggested documents.

After finalizing your plans, explain to your children exactly what you have put in your will. Let them ask any questions and express their concerns. Your openness will help them accept the decisions you have made.

Sense of Entitlement

Another problem that crops up in blended families is children's attitudes toward what parents and stepparents owe them. Many times unreal expectations develop.

For instance, when LaDean and I married, I owned a house I had received in the divorce settlement. Six months later, I chose to sell the property.

"Dad," David informed me, "Paul and I were told that any profit from selling that house would belong to us."

"Who ever told you that?" I asked, upset. "That's certainly not the case."

Disappointed, David immediately told Paul who also felt he had been wronged. Their bitterness lasted for several years.

A sense of entitlement can crop up in many situations. Kids commonly come home from a visit with the ex-husband and ask, "Where is all the money Daddy sends you each month?" Or they want to know, "Why don't you give me as much allowance as Dad does?"

Our friends, Jim and Becky Ownby, experienced a classic situation. Jim's sixteen-year-old son, who lived with his mother, began having engine trouble with his pickup. Jim helped him fix it several times.

One day, the son informed his dad, "I want a new pickup."

"Son, I just can't afford it."

The young man huffed, "Well, you should have planned better."

Children who don't have the continuity of one family situation often develop a sense of entitlement which builds over time. For instance, an absent father wants to give his kids something and since he cannot share his time, he buys them things. He feels this is the only way he can show his love.

Or Mother sees her ex-husband showering the kids with toys and gifts. She is afraid they will want to be with their father more than with her, so she gives them a bigger allowance and lets them stay up later. What the children learn is that Mom and Dad always seem to have goodies for them. They never understand the limitations of a budget.

In another situation, a newlywed wife demands that her husband buy the same gifts for her children as he does for his own. Consequently, his kids feel less important because they think the stepbrothers and stepsisters are replacing them in the family. So they complain to their father who then expects his wife to provide for his children in the same way she has given to her own. And the cycle continues.

We suggest that parents carefully set spending policies. For example, plan Christmas lists carefully so you don't add to sibling rivalry. Agree to avoid competing for children's love by buying gifts or doling out money. Bring children into the budget process so they better understand why you refuse certain purchases. And give each child special treats or gifts while making sure that no one person receives more attention than another.

Partnership in Giving

"I want a stereo, a bunch of new outfits to wear to school and some decent earrings," Janna announced three weeks before her birthday.

Carol stared at her stepdaughter in disbelief. "That's quite a list!"

"All the other kids at school get what they want on their birthdays. Jody and Theresa give their parents huge lists."

Later, Carol and her new husband Wayne discussed Janna's requests. "I guess I've always made too much of birthdays," he admitted. "But I felt guilty about her mother leaving us years ago."

Carol nodded. "All of us have gotten into the habit of wanting too many things. What can we do to change?"

Materialism, territorial feelings about possessions

and an unwillingness to share with new family members all plague many blended families. These blended family dynamics play havoc with the process of bonding. How can we counteract habits and desires that have a divisive impact on family life? By developing a family financial plan which includes gifts and giving.

Our Lord says, "It is more blessed to give than to receive" (Acts 20:35, NIV). When we give freely of ourselves and of our material assets, our focus changes. We begin looking for others' needs. We share in the joys and triumphs of watching our money accomplish things for God that we never expected.

We encourage you to set aside a certain percentage of your income for the Lord's work and to look for opportunities to help others in financial difficulties. You will be surprised how giving will begin to build a generous and unselfish atmosphere in your home.

Planning for the future will bring lasting rewards. You will settle some of the delicate issues ahead of time that can cause irreparable damage during a crisis. Making a budget will help you set priorities and understand the needs and desires of your mate. Writing a will can give you assurance for the future and help untangle the web of obligations and expectations you bring to your relationship. And learning to give will open your hearts to the Lord's leading and open your home to God's grace.

We would like to suggest some guidelines that may help you plan your financial future and set spending policies:

1. If you are planning marriage, prepare a budget and write a will before your wedding.

   If you are newly married, prepare the budget and write a will as soon as possible, preferably in the first month.

   If you are already married, prepare the budget and write a will when things are good between you, even if you fear rocking the boat. The long-range results are worth it.

2. Prepare separate budgets and share your ideas at an appointed time and place. After coming to a consensus, sleep on your decisions and discuss your budget again in a day or two. Don't make the process all-consuming. Set a structure for finishing your work, honor it and go about normal living.

3. Begin each part of this process with prayer. Be sensitive to the Lord's leading in what is best for your family. Pray for an open mind, a willing heart and God's wisdom.

4. When discussing your budget, stay on the subject and use conciliation, negotiation and compromise. Make a rule that no other issue or frustration can be brought up at this time.

5. Your local Christian bookstore or church library will have material to help you understand finances and giving.

6. Take a financial management class offered through an adult education program at a local high school, college or business.

7. Consult professionals familiar with blended family experiences for financial complications that go beyond your expertise. Seek advice from an attorney, financial advisor, insurance agent or accountant.

8. As circumstances change, take time to adjust your budget.

9. Use the same process mentioned in #2 and #3 to write your will. Seek the expertise of an attorney after your preliminary discussion.

10. When you have finished making your budget

and writing your will, thank God for helping you plan wisely and treat yourselves to something special.

None of this can be accomplished without God's wisdom. Solomon writes, "Wisdom is a shelter as money is a shelter, but the advantages of knowledge is this: that wisdom preserves the life of its possessor" (Ecclesiastes 7:12, NIV). Dealing with financial matters with godly wisdom also protects the life of a marriage. We urge you to seek God first in handling your money matters. Seeking His will allows you to pass many financial obstacles without incident and gain a closer, more intimate fellowship with each other.

MAKING OF A MIRACLE

As a couple, examine the options presented and decide which ones best complement your goals. What we consider right and fair for us may not work for you. For this reason, we have not given you rules to live by, but we would suggest some guidelines that may help you as you move toward your solutions.

1. Use the basic budget worksheet provided here to list current and future expenses and compare results. You may wish to be more detailed than we have been.

2. Make a plan for financial freedom which includes paying off credit cards and agreeing not to make new unnecessary purchases. Make a commitment to follow your plan.

SUGGESTED BUDGET FORM

Item	Current Amount	Future Amount
Tithe	_____	_____
Housing	_____	_____
Automobile	_____	_____
Food	_____	_____
Clothing	_____	_____
Medical	_____	_____
Insurance	_____	_____
Taxes	_____	_____
Entertainment	_____	_____
Outstanding Debts	_____	_____
Savings	_____	_____
Miscellaneous	_____	_____
TOTALS	_____	_____

Compare your
Income _____
minus -
Current Expenses _____

TOTAL _____

to
Income _____
minus -
Future Expenses _____

TOTAL _____

Blend for the week of _____

Until you are willing to share your money, you are
not willing to share your life.

For where your treasure is, there will your heart be also.
(Matthew 6:21, NAS)

*Blessings for the week of*_____

13

Removing Locked Doorknobs

Don

LaDean and I slept in late one lazy Saturday morning about two weeks after we were married. I lay half-dozing, enjoying her warm presence beside me. Rays of sunlight filtered through the curtains and danced on her hair.

Suddenly, she raised her head off the pillow and whispered, "What's that noise?"

We both stared at our locked bedroom door. The knob began to turn gently. Then everything was silent.

She looked at me. "Must be Trey trying to get in. Ten-year-olds hate to be left out of anything."

I grinned. "Locks come in handy sometimes."

The doorknob clattered again. "What's he doing now?" Her voice held a bit of irritation.

"He's removing the knob."

"He knows he's not supposed to disturb us when the door is locked."

I shook my head. "Let's not scold him. This is something precious. I think he just wants to be a part of our family." The doorknob moved up and down loosely. LaDean started chuckling, her motions wiggling the mattress. Suddenly, both of us burst into uncontrollable laughter.

One more rattle and the doorknob fell onto the carpet with a dull thud. Trey cautiously peeked in the door dressed in his pajamas, holding a big red screwdriver.

LaDean motioned him to the bed. "Come on in." Setting the tool on the dresser, he jumped in between us and snuggled down under the covers. LaDean and I moved closer.

Few relationships in life bring more joy than parenting. It requires great effort, but we gladly pay the price to see our children grow up happy and healthy.

Sometimes, however, relationships in blended families resemble locked rooms in a house. Each person lives in his own space and doesn't reach out to the stranger who is now part of his world. He resists any attempt by others to invade his territory. We can help remove locked doors and build unobstructed love and acceptance in our children. But this takes a firm commitment to godly parenting.

The Acceptance Process

Other than our relationship with the Lord and our spouse, raising children in a blended family demands more from us than anything else we do. New personality dynamics create divisions and conflicts. Expectations brought by both partners into the marriage can change when children move in. Let's look at the stresses encountered by different members of the family in this situation.

First, the stepparent (the blended parent) feels the need to correct the young strangers living with him. Often he objects to the rules and policies of his mate, or he has natural children who complicate relationships. He also feels deeply about his own contribution to parenting which may not be accepted by the blended children.

Second, the natural parent tries to defend and protect his sons and daughters against new family members. He resists changing parenting practices he used in the past, especially if they worked well. Since he thinks he knows his child better than anyone else, he resents a new partner trying to tell him how to raise his own offspring. Guilt fed by an ex-mate causes the natural parent to give the children what they want, to fight their battles for them and to try to relieve the youngsters' pain. This indulgence further strains the relationship between the blended parent and the children.

Third, the child has been thrust into a situation where he believes he has lost control. His family life has been shattered, and everything familiar is being reconstructed. He is expected to obey the instructions of an unfamiliar person and feels confused by the new set of expectations. At the same time, he receives pressure from his absent parent who wants his child to love and prefer him above the blended parent. The child is showered with gifts and money and expects his natural parent to fund his independence with no questions asked.

How many of these conflicts are present in your home? Are you aware of how these issues divide your family? How can two people who are trying to bond resolve problems with children too?

Your family relationships will not blossom until you and your mate bond as a couple. A powerful principle is at work here: There has to be an ending before there can be a new beginning. The ending is that a former relationship has died, but the bonding of the newly blended parents will bring a positive response out of that death.

It will give rise to the new beginning and it will help the children progress through their own stages of blending more easily and with less stress.

Children go through several stages in learning to accept a blended parent—regardless of age or whether they live at home or on their own. A child can get stuck in any one of the stages for any period of time, especially a son or daughter who lives outside the home. We were first introduced to these stages by Brooke Annis, our counselor.

Through a process of acceptance, each family member can dismantle those locked doorknobs. Each child moves through the five stages at his or her own pace.

1. Combination

In the combination stage, the child dislikes the blended parent and believes this person has invaded OUR house. When this stranger begins giving directions, they sound too much like orders and the child thinks, *Who gave him the right to tell me what to do?* Usually, the blended child will react by being neutral. He will feel this stage is the most comfortable because he does not have to make a commitment to the family relationship. When encouraged to interact, he may say, "I don't like my new stepdad." Or he may respond to questions or suggestions with a shrug and an, "I don't know."

2. Suspicion

My oldest son, David, was twenty-one years old when his mother and I divorced. At twenty-six, he confessed, "For several years after you and Mom split, I dreamed that you would get back together. I desperately wanted us to be a family again."

I was shocked. I hadn't realized how much he wanted to see us reunited.

Children naturally blame themselves for the

breakup of their family. This guilt is a heavy burden. Like David, they fantasize about living as one family.

When Mom or Dad remarries, the child's dream is shattered. He blames the newcomer for ruining the fantasy. This wish is a powerful force, especially if used against the blended parent. Often the child reacts in a hostile manner.

The ex-spouse may add confusion by playing the "poor me" game and telling his son or daughter, "I love you so much, but we don't get to spend time together anymore because you are always with your [blended parent]."

Since blended parents go through these same stages, the adults and children both can get stuck in this stage for an indefinite period. To prevent this, the natural parent must gently help the children deal with their hostility toward the blended parent and encourage them to release their broken dreams.

3. Aloofness

Children in the aloofness stage have little or no reaction to the blended parent and raise the absent parent to instant sainthood. Because so much attention and effort is lavished on the children, the blended adult feels abandoned. At the same time, the divorced parent feels left out of his former family. As a result, resentments can easily develop.

Children display aloofness by asking the natural parent to relay information to the blended parent when he is standing right there. To keep harmony, the adults go along. Not only does indirect communication allow the children to continue their indifference, but many times it also divides the parents.

How do you remedy this situation? The natural parent lovingly declines the role of go-between and insists that the child address the blended parent.

This happened in our family. Trey said to LaDean, "Mom, tell Don I need some paper for school."

She replied wisely, "Trey, if you would like him to know that, you'll need to tell him yourself. He's right here." Once Trey observed our solidarity, he had a greater desire to join our family unit.

But don't rush closeness. Instead, gently encourage each child's effort to join your circle of love. That's why we brought Trey into our bed that Saturday morning. We realized that unscrewing the doorknob showed his desire to be a part of us. When we welcomed him, we reaffirmed his position in the family. Our acceptance encouraged him to "break in" and move with freedom into the readiness stage.

Later we had him replace the doorknob, and he learned about rebuilding something that had been taken apart. How timely for all of us!

4. Readiness

In this stage, the children accept the blended parent as a real person. They initiate conversations and treat him as an acquaintance though they haven't yet developed strong ties.

Often Trey would walk in between us when we were going somewhere or would squeeze into our circle when LaDean and I were hugging. I chose to make this a blending rather than a separating action. Rather than push him away, I would growl loudly and pick both of them off the floor. We called this our "love monster hug."

We feel that children will hesitate to progress through the stages if they fear the couple will not stay together. They often will even regress in the stages because they don't want to let themselves like the blended parent if they are going to lose that person. This is why we feel bonding is the foundation of the family structure.

Because children in this stage aren't sure how much

of their natural parent they will have in the future, they test the couple's relationship. They want to know if their parents' new bond has enough security to accept childhood behavior in a positive way. The parents, as the bond strengthens, can accept these testings, and the family unity can grow.

5. Acceptance

At this stage, children welcome the blended parent as a partner to Mom or Dad and as having some kind of relationship with themselves. By accepting each other as full members of the family, parents and children begin building a secure atmosphere that withstands the stresses and crises of family living. Each person begins to express himself and rely on other family members for support.

Cultivating a deeper relationship depends on many factors, primarily the openness of both the children and the natural parent and blended parent, and the permanency of the marriage. Children will hesitate to accept the blended parent if they fear that the couple will break up.

Don't become discouraged if someone in your family regresses when going through one of these stages. This is quite normal. Your gentle encouragement will help your children progress to greater acceptance with less stress. As they change, commit yourself to changing with them.

Adults also go through the process of acceptance. The process of becoming a successful blended parent is similar to that of selecting a seeing-eye dog. Since the person who is getting the dog is blind, he cannot see to select it. I was told once that the blind person is placed in a particular area and the dogs are brought in one at a time. The process is completed when a dog selects the person.

The adult will need to initiate closeness without forcing movement through the stages. LaDean describes how she handled our situation.

LaDean

Initiating Acceptance

After Don and I married, I decided to take a low profile with his sons. *Let them come to me*, I thought.

After some time, I realized that initiating the relationship was my responsibility. I should have poise, gentleness and quiet strength, not create more chaos with wrongful attitudes. So I began consciously building a relationship with David and Paul.

This past Father's Day, my decision was tested.

David and his family were leaving after a Father's Day dinner. As he hugged me, he turned to his father. "Good-bye, Dad." Then he spoke to me. "And goodbye . . . " he paused, "whatever you are."

His remark could have offended me, but I realized this was his way of accepting me so I replied, "I'll take 'friend.' " He smiled and nodded. I knew that "friend" can be the ultimate compliment in a blended family.

If you are a blended parent, patiently wait for your blended child to accept you. Don't let feelings of guilt and failure upset his progress, especially if he seems to regress or move too slowly. Let him set the pace. In time, you will see the results of your patience and quiet persistence.

One year, Don and I attended his end-of-the-year athletic banquet. I sat with the dean of girls and her husband, who was Trey's high school history teacher.

He described a class discussion they'd had recently. "Some of the students told stories about how bad their stepparents were. Without undue criticism, I encouraged them to express their feelings. In the middle of the discussion, Trey piped up, 'My stepdad's not like that at all. He's cool.' "

That's acceptance.

MAKING OF A MIRACLE

To begin the process of restructuring your parenting, we suggest you take an inventory of where each member in your immediate and extended family is in relation to the Stages of Blended Children.

Once you have determined where you are, ask the Lord for guidance in whatever changes He wants to make in you. Then ask for strength as you initiate changes in the pressures your children have been feeling.

Remember how important it is to allow people the freedom to adjust to these changes at their own pace.

Blend for the week of _____

It takes special people to be parents.

Just as a father has compassion on his children, so the
LORD has compassion on those who fear Him.
(Psalm 103:13, NAS)

*Blessings for the week of*_____

```
┌─────────────────────────────────┐
│      DETOUR–ROUGH               │
│      PAVEMENT                   │
└─────────────────────────────────┘
```

14

Power Parenting

Don

Recall the last vacation you took as a family by car? Though you were excited as you pulled out of the driveway, many hours later, tiredness and irritation set in. The road seemed to go on forever. And the kids were in the back seat arguing about who gets to play with which toy.

Suddenly a sign looms on the right: "Detour—Rough Pavement."

"Oh, no," you groan. *How long with this take? Will I have to turn back and retrace my route? Have I taken a wrong turn?*

As blended parents, we, too, can discover rough pavement in parenting. These detours cause dissension, incomplete bonding and friction. But with careful handling, they will add richness to your family life. LaDean begins with the dangers of parental competition.

LaDean
_____

Building a Relationship With Natural Parents

When Don and I dated, I wasn't communicating with my ex-husband about Trey. Trey was to spend the weekend with his dad after our wedding. When my ex-husband came to the door, I decided, *This is a good time to introduce him to Don.* After all, wouldn't a parent want to meet the adult their child would be living with?

The three of us stood in the front doorway. I began, "This is my husband . . . "

Suddenly, Trey's dad interrupted in a loud voice, "I don't want to have anything to do with him!"

Don looked at both of us in disbelief. The neighbors were treated to some wonderful Saturday night entertainment, and I was shocked. I figured the three of us would get along easily.

We all have come a long way since then. That was brought home to me one day on a return flight from a speaking engagement in Houston. I sat next to a nice man in the thirty-something age group and as we talked, he asked, "How did you and your ex-husband get to the point where you could talk about your child and make decisions about him without fighting?"

For a moment, I couldn't answer. Scenes from the past eight years flew through my mind.

As he asked me one question after another and as I described our experiences, I realized he was taking me through the steps the three of us had gone through to build our unique relationship. I explained, "My husband and Trey's father and I all feel comfortable sharing my son's activities, honors and experiences."

The man was amazed. "You have a one-of-a-kind family."

His astonishment made me grateful for the harmony Trey enjoys. The good relationship between the adults in his life has relieved him of the pressure of choosing between us and allowed him to live in freedom. Since all of us communicate about parenting, we have closed the exit doors for Trey—he can't pit one of us against the other.

We encourage the natural parents to bring out the best qualities in the relationship you now have. Respect each other's feelings and rights and put aside the wrongs and hardships. The well-being of your child depends on how you react and respond to your ex-mate's involvement in your child's life.

A blended parent will have more success in bonding with his new family if he supports the relationship each child has with his natural parent, whether absent or present.

Dealing With Authority Issues

The subject of authority in blended families raises some unique conflicts.

First, children come into the new home with established expectations of authority. In a single parent family, a child, especially a boy, often sees himself as the "man" of the house. He assumes as many duties as he can handle—and even some he can't. An identical situation develops when a daughter lives with her dad. She takes on many of the duties of her mother. The devastation of a divorce or death can cloud the sensitivity of parents to their children's needs as they work at surviving their loss.

When the natural parent remarries, the role the child has assumed is often forgotten in the excitement, and he is suddenly expected to act like a child again. He resents the change. His indignation soon turns to anger—and the adults are mystified at his radically different behavior.

A couple in one of our seminars told us this story.

They remarried after being single for several years. She had a teenage son who was enthusiastic about the relationship before the wedding, but after the ceremony, his behavior deteriorated.

For several months, the couple tried to talk to the son. He would not open up to them.

One day, the mother and the young man were arguing about something, and she said to him, "You have rebelled against us ever since the wedding!"

The teenager broke into tears. "But you never asked me if you could get married!"

She looked at her tall, lanky son. He had been the man of the house for years. He felt he had protected and cared for her.

She put her arms around him and said, "I'm so sorry, honey. I really blew it, didn't I? I didn't give you a chance to be part of this big decision." She pulled back and looked him in the eyes. "Can you forgive me?"

"Of course, I forgive you, Mom."

Immediately, the relationships in the family began to heal. This family found it beneficial to redefine the roles of each family member so the son could enjoy the opportunity of being a child again.

When you see behavior changes in a child, keep the lines of communication open. Your children will be healthier if you help them grow at a normal pace and not allow them to load themselves down with heavy burdens.

Another authority issue is, how much should the blended parent discipline the child?

We found it necessary to give verbal permission. In front of my son I told Don, "I give you the authority to discipline Trey." Saying the words was the easy part. The challenge was not stepping in when Don began to correct Trey. We made a decision early in our marriage to disagree privately about discipline rather than fight about this issue in front of Trey.

Don helped by working with me in the discipline process. He explains how.

Don

When LaDean first gave me the right to discipline Trey, his face blanched. He saw this big, fierce, 225-pound person given authority over him, and he did not know exactly what the limits were. I believe a little bit of wonderment can be beneficial at times, although it should not be fear. What we did not tell him in detail was we had discussed the *limits to my discipline.* We had agreed I would not physically discipline Trey. In the beginning, LaDean felt I would spank him too hard, and I really did not feel it was my right to physically discipline him.

I feel even more strongly now that the blended parent must limit his role in discipline as well as in other decisions concerning the blended child. Since LaDean has always done a great job in raising Trey, I never felt the need to bring stronger restraint into our home. Instead, I have tried to act as supporter and advisor to LaDean and to Trey's natural father. This has been the best role for me, and it has allowed us all to develop a relationship full of trust and unselfishness.

LaDean shares some of the techniques to use to minimize conflict.

LaDean

A United Front

A blended couple should be together in the areas of household rules, finances, spiritual life, and in presenting a united front to the children and to the outside world. These may include curfew, chores, respect for others, common courtesy and many others. They can vary greatly depending on what you decide is comfortable for all of you.

We suggest that you take time to set fair and workable policies and routines. Allow each child to participate in the discussion. Write down what you have decided and periodically review how each rule is working in family life.

Another dimension of the unified front involves the inclusion of the absent, natural parent. The more the absent parent is included in policy making involving the child, the more secure the child feels.

When It Comes to Money . . .

Giving money to children usually poses special problems for blended parents. Children will take advantage of parental disagreement or lack of communication.

We had an interesting experience with Trey in his junior year in high school.

Unknown to me, Don had given him twenty dollars for a date after his band concert. Before he left, I asked, "Do you need any money?"

"Sure," he replied enthusiastically.

I gave him ten dollars.

After the concert, Trey's dad, Don and I stopped to talk. I turned to Trey's dad. "Did you give Trey any money?"

"Yes, twenty dollars."

Don piped up, "Well, I gave him twenty, too."

"And I handed him ten," I added.

The next morning, I confronted Trey. "Did you have any change left over from last night?"

"Well . . . My date cost twelve dollars, and you only gave me ten."

"What did you do with the two twenties your dad and Don gave you?"

His expression was priceless.

I looked him straight in the eye. "You agreed to tell your dad and me when the other one had given you money. Because you did not do this, we've decided to keep each other informed."

The next evening, Don, Trey's dad and I were waiting when Trey came home from church. As he walked in the door, he saw the three of us sitting together. "What are you all doing here?"

I spoke up. "We're waiting to discuss your new economy. We want your input on how much money you need."

Trey sat down.

We discovered that Trey had been getting about three hundred dollars a month with no obligations. His dad finally suggested, "Trey, we'll give you a week to come up with a proposed budget. Then we'll decide on an allowance."

The next Sunday, the four of us met to determine a budget and what Trey would be responsible for. From this we determined an appropriate allowance, and decided to open a checking account for him. Our desire was for him to learn to manage his money while he was still at home and willing to learn from us.

Because we worked together, Trey learned several lessons from this experience, including how to handle money and the importance of communicating.

You, too, can use this potentially touchy area to build better understanding. No teen likes to have his spending restricted, but in time he will appreciate the abilities he gains through disciplined spending and he will see more clearly the value of family agreements.

Understanding the Role of Grandparents

Grandparents play an important role in the process of acceptance—that of support. Their contribution to children's self-esteems can be invaluable, when they put aside their feelings about "the past."

Don and I have seen a disturbing trend in blended families. Many times the grandparents on the absent parent's side are virtually eliminated from the child's life.

My ex-husband's mother shared a sad experience with me the day Trey graduated from high school. She sat next to a woman whose son and daughter-in-law had divorced. With tears in her eyes, the woman said, "I have not seen or spoken to my granddaughter in five years. I do not know how tall she is, how she is doing in school or even if she remembers me." Who can describe the loss for both the older woman and the little girl?

That day, Trey's grandmother's face glowed. "I appreciate so much the way you have included me in Trey's life."

I can't describe how wonderful that made me feel. Not only had I allowed her to share with Trey, but he was the richer for having the relationship with her. I am grateful to the Lord for giving me the desire to forgive and the compassion to understand other people's feelings.

We must be careful not to scar our children by getting in the way of a healthy relationship with their grandparents. I am thankful that the Lord showed me this truth when Trey was still a child. This helped me give my child access to his natural grandparents.

Many grandparents engage in manipulative actions which isolate them from their loved ones. Some put down the parents or deride the new marriage to a grandchild. This drives the child closer to the parent being attacked who may keep the child away from the grandparent. If the parent being attacked is the blended parent, these actions will feed the child's natural resistance to the blended parent. Resist the temptation to engage in such harmful activities. Instead, help your grandchildren adjust to the new circumstances in their lives.

Avoid creating competition between you and other grandparents. Now that I'm a grandmother, I have to watch what I say.

The other day, I picked up my granddaughter from kindergarten. "Kalese, let's have lunch together."

She smiled, pleased.

As we were eating, she spoke proudly, "Gramis, I sure have a lot of grandmothers."

I put my hand over hers. "Yes, Kalese, you do have a lot of grandmothers, and we all love you very much. Isn't it neat to be special to so many people?"

Her face beamed.

How innocent and vulnerable she is, I suddenly realized. *It would be easy to tell her I love her more than the others do.* Or, if I had been the natural grandmother, I could have said, "Yes, but your other grandma is not really your grandmother."

It's so tempting to make factual but destructive remarks. The long-term impact on her trusting heart could create a lifetime of doubt and unstable relationships. My focus must be on her mental health, not on my opinions or on any competition for her affection.

Often grandparents' roles change when a remarriage takes place. Sometimes, they must relinquish the position of mother or father figure to the child. How hard it is to give up such closeness! Remembering what is best for the child will keep you from holding on too tightly.

Are you wondering how you can put all these suggestions together? We have developed some guidelines to help you. Remember, our power in parenting is the power of the Holy Spirit. We call them our Steps for Power Parenting.

Steps for Power Parenting

1. *Make a firm decision to help your children become mentally and emotionally healthy.* My first goal was for Trey to grow into a healthy young man, but he could not do this in the middle of a power struggle. As teachers, Don and I saw the end result of teenagers caught in this kind of dilemma when their parents divorced. Sometimes children are allowed to move from one house to another whenever they feel pressure. This creates insecurity and unstable relationships.

2. *Focus your attention on your children, not on getting back at an ex-mate.* Every parent has tender feelings about his child. Use that healthy emotion to overcome your desire for revenge. Open the lines of communication.

3. *You begin the communication process.* How do you start? You decide that the children are so valuable that it's worth it for you to be the initiator. If necessary, try again and again until your ex-spouse begins communicating concerning the children.

Don and I began by meeting for breakfast at a neighborhood restaurant with Trey's dad. A public place was neutral turf and caused us to be nicer to each other. This method worked very well for us.

4. *Focus your conversation on the welfare of the child.* I found that working from a prepared agenda forced me to stay on the subject—Trey—and helped show his dad that I was not "after" him.

In the beginning, I had to remind myself constantly that my focus was on Trey, not myself. As I practiced thinking about my son first, it became more natural. It was necessary *for me* to say to Trey's dad, "I want us to work together on this."

5. *As a blended parent, support the natural parent's efforts to communicate.* Remember that you have an advisory position but you must allow the natural parents to make the decisions concerning the child.

6. As the natural parent, seriously consider the advice of the blended parent. Because the decisions will affect everyone, the natural parent should let the blended parent know his advice has been considered.

7. As a blended parent, build up the relationship between the natural parents and the children. Natural parents, do the same for the blended parent and your son or daughter. This can be an opportunity to bond as a couple or it can be an opportunity to cause division between the couple. The outcome is the couple's choice.

8. As a blended parent, make a conscious effort to involve yourself with the blended children. How do you do this? By becoming interested in what the child is doing. Your concern makes him feel you want to be part of his life.

9. Pray for all involved again and again and again. Claim the verse, "Pray without ceasing" (1 Thessalonians 5:17, NIV). Begin with prayer to make your heart right with the Lord, then ask Him to help you restore communication with your ex-spouse. Pray as a couple as well as individually. Children will also benefit from being included in the praying process.

By now I'm sure you have concluded that bonding and building relationships take commitment, work and staying power. But the rewards! We could never describe how rich our lives have become and how much we are looking forward to many more years together. How about you? Have you begun your journey?

You will be amazed at the spiritual, mental and emotional benefits you will reap from power parenting. And what's more, we are confident that you will enjoy the trip!

MAKING OF A MIRACLE

Whether you're parents or grandparents, we urge you to desire the mental health of the children. Realize that children learn more from what they see than what they hear. *You are their model!*

Set aside some time this weekend with your natural children and some time with your blended children. This does not necessarily have to be something extravagant, but can just be a "together time." We earnestly pray for you as you focus on the Blend Card for this chapter and seek to make positive changes in your family.

Blend for the week of _____

It is easier to build children than to repair adults.

> *[Parents], do not exasperate your children that*
> *they may not lose heart.*
> (Colossians 3:21, NAS)

Blessings for the week of _____

15

Woman to Woman: The Closets of Your Heart

LaDean

On our wedding day, Don moved into my house. I had seven closets, two of which belonged to Trey. The other five I had filled with my things.

Don walked into the house with one suitcase as if he were just spending the night. Motioning toward a corner of our bedroom, I said, "You can put your bag over there on the floor. I'll empty a closet for you later."

And so Don began to take socks, shirts and pants from his suitcase in the morning and return them in the evening. By the end of the second month, he was irritated. "When are you going to get around to giving me a place to put my clothes? I'm tired of living out of my suitcase."

That weekend, I cleaned out half of my smallest closet and removed my things from one dresser drawer—

all the while muttering, "He should be grateful. I'm so busy, I just don't have time to spend rearranging things."

Later I realized why I didn't give him room in my closet. I wanted him to be packed and ready to leave at any moment. Unconsciously, I had been setting up situations which would allow him to leave if he wanted to. I didn't trust Don with my heart or believe that God would protect the marriage He had given me. Because of the scars of a broken relationship, I was afraid of the big "C" word—*commitment*. Letting Don have a drawer and closet space seemed like I was opening my heart to give him a permanent place.

What kind of heart are you giving your husband? Is it wounded, willing, washed or welcoming? Is it cleaned and rearranged, giving him space to settle in? Or is your heart so wounded that you keep the doors to your emotions and commitment partially closed?

The Wounded Heart

Sometimes, we do not give our partner the best of ourselves. If we are still carrying hurt, pain, guilt, despair, hate or unforgiveness, we offer our husband a wounded heart.

We all enter marriage with expectations of living happily ever after—even the second time around. But since we have come through the pain of a broken relationship, we have tender places and tough scars within us that make us hesitant to open ourselves to someone new. We view our new relationship through a wounded heart.

But hanging onto our brokenness will not allow us to reach the level of intimacy we would like to have. We set ourselves up for a wounded relationship.

What have you hidden in the closets of your hearts that will affect the level of intimacy? Can you share the hidden wounds? Or have you blocked off parts of yourself from your new partner?

I urge you to begin searching the inner hurts that mar your mental health and the well-being of your family. I have found that Jesus is a friend who will heal your pain and fears. And He is just a prayer away. Claim and continue to apply Psalm 139:23,24: "Search me O God, and know my heart . . . see if there be any hurtful way in me" (NAS). Then open the locked closets of your heart to your marriage partner, and let him have a permanent place in your emotions and spirit. Begin by offering him a willing heart.

The Willing Heart

Counseling sessions and classes on divorce recovery helped me get over most of the effects of my divorce. I remember discussing trust and submission, but I think I was putting so much energy into becoming whole again that I wasn't ready to concentrate on these subjects.

One of my instructors said, "LaDean, you *will* trust again."

I immediately replied, "I'll never trust anyone in a close relationship again. Or let myself to be hurt like that a second time."

"Yes, you will. One day you'll experience love."

Maybe some people, but not me!

My instructor was right. In time, I did heal enough to open myself up to another person. I became more willing to trust after the day Don slammed his fist on the kitchen counter and said, "I don't care what you do. I am not leaving."

What a relief! All this time I thought he was going to end this marriage every time we disagreed. If he was going to stay with me regardless of what I did, then I really could trust him. And I could trust God to be there for us when we experienced the trials and tribulations that blended family living brings. I thought, *Maybe the best is yet to be. Can I allow myself this happiness?*

I remember what the marriage counselor told me before Don and I married. I had gone to him because I was unsure of getting married again. He asked me to describe the worst thing that could happen. I said that D-I-V-O-R-C-E was the worst thing that could happen. He asked if I could handle that. I told him I guessed I could, but I didn't want to. He said, "Why not take a chance? You just might be happy."

If Don wasn't going to leave, I just might be happy. My heart was beginning to be willing to feel, trust and give again.

As women, we sometimes let our expectations interfere with a developing relationship. We are not willing to give up what we think should happen for what actually will take place. Our narrow concept closes our heart to the ones we love.

Are you offering your husband a willing heart? Proverbs 23:7 reminds us, "For as a man [or woman] thinketh in his heart, so is he." We will never rise above our own expectations. Once you have begun the process of giving yourself to another person, you will need to set realistic expectations, which may mean setting new expectations for yourself, your spouse and your family.

What can you expect in a blended family? You will not find absolute, exact answers, nor will you find "realistic" to be the same for each family.

I must admit that when Don and I first married, I didn't think too much about expectations. Somehow that subject took the romance out of the moment. But underneath, I nurtured fairy-tale dreams.

For example, I saw us as a big happy family. Though I never wanted to take the place of David and Paul's mother, or even to be called "Mom," I figured Don's boys would welcome me with open arms, and David, Paul and Trey would love each other like brothers. Don and I would advise and care for them.

It didn't take long for my bubble to burst!

Two days after our honeymoon, our church choir participated in a Christmas special at the mall. We drove my car.

After the concert, we joyfully returned to the parking lot. Suddenly, I spied something wrong. "Don, my gas cap's missing!" I panicked. "How can we drive my car? Do you think someone's filled my gas tank with sugar or sand? We'll ruin the engine."

He checked it out and thought it was safe to drive home.

The next morning, I discovered someone had spray-painted my blue car with black paint. Since Don's ex-wife had been at the mall at the same time we were, I jumped to the conclusion that she was behind all this.

I was naive enough to think that David and Paul would be as upset as I was over the damage to my car. After all, didn't they enjoy driving it? Now that I was their new stepmother, shouldn't they be more concerned about what happens to me? Even Don wasn't as worried as I thought he should be.

I have since realized that the boys' "ho-hum" attitude was their way of keeping out of a problem that was not really theirs. Even if their mother had done something, how could they take my side against her?

My expectations were not realistic in this situation or in many other things that have happened since. My desire was to have one big happy family. I had to be willing to clean out my unrealistic expectations and replace them with practical goals. Each of us brought limitations and scars into the relationship that would make rebuilding family life much different from what I expected.

I urge you to uncover the expectations you have carried into your new relationship. Some can be subtle and hard to detect. But unless you recognize and alter the unrealistic ones, they will interfere with the closeness you are trying to build.

Another part of the closet we have to clean out is our unwillingness to submit. This word brings up lots of controversy when mentioned in our blended family workshops. I know my own definition of submission in marriage was distorted when I remarried. Every time Don told me I was not submissive, I got angry.

How could I yield to him when I could not trust that he would stay in our marriage? Submission is not instant; we have to work into it. You don't receive a spirit of submission the moment you walk down the aisle and say, "I do" and "I will."

One woman's explanation of submission was especially appealing to me. She said, "It is ducking low enough and fast enough to let the Lord hit your husband in the head." I'm not sure that is on target theologically, but I remember wishing many times that the Lord would hit Don in the head! Maybe this is what it means when we allow our husbands the freedom to fail rather than try to rescue them. It is important for us to be supportive of them when they have failed.

The Bible uses vivid pictures to explain how submission works in marriage. I like the way Ephesians describes the husband/wife relationship:

> Wives, be subject to your own husbands, as to the Lord. For the husband is the head of the wife, as Christ also is the head of the church . . . But as the church is subject to Christ, so also the wives ought to be to their husbands in everything (Ephesians 5:22-24, NAS).

I like to think of the husband/wife relationship as a head/body relationship. When the body hurts, so does the head. One part cannot survive without the other. Both are necessary for effective operation. As wives, we submit to our husbands, not as a lesser person but as a working half that makes an essential contribution.

First Peter 3:7 refers to a joint-heir relationship. Each spouse is a "fellow heir in the grace of life" (NAS). This means we are equal in God's scheme of glory, both in heaven and on earth. When we are on-line with Him, the submission thing takes care of itself. We don't have to concentrate; it just happens.

To keep from getting in the way of it "just happening," I have to remind myself of 1 Peter 3:4: "Let it be the hidden person of the heart, with the imperishable quality of a gentle and quiet spirit, which is precious in the sight of God" (NAS). When I cultivate a gentle spirit, I more easily yield my "right of way" to Don's direction.

The Washed Heart

Are you ready to offer your mate a washed heart?

We begin to clean our hearts just like we clean our closets. Our closets are usually places where we store items, but sometimes we stash trash or hide things there. We must not use our hearts in this way.

The Bible tells us that the Lord will wash our hearts. The apostle Paul writes, "[Christ will] sanctify [the church], having cleansed her by the washing of water with the word" (Ephesians 5:26, NAS).

As the Lord strips away all our undesirables, it can hurt. But when He removes something, He fills the void with Himself. He becomes a soothing balm for your heart. He did this for me through His Word, renewed relationships, positive change in my life and a desire to know more of Him. Sometimes I have felt totally alone with nowhere to turn, and I found Him there. I had to bottom out in my relationship with Don to be willing to be cleansed. The exciting part of being cleansed is that I get to begin again.

I like to meditate on Psalm 51:10-12. I catch myself singing these words many times a day:

> *Create* in me a clean heart, O God,
> And *renew* a steadfast spirit within me.
> Do not cast me away from Thy presence,

And do not take Thy Holy Spirit from me.
Restore to me the joy of Thy salvation,
And *sustain* me with a willing spirit (NAS).

The cycle of create, renew, restore, sustain is like the cycle of a marriage. Don and I have experienced a cleansing in writing this book and have found so much healing. How exciting when we discover that we are becoming what we were meant to be!

I encourage you to allow the Lord to wash your heart. We must bathe every part of our lives, even the most incidental area, in prayer. During trying moments, claim 1 Peter 5:10:

After you have suffered for a little while, the God of all grace, who called you to His eternal glory in Christ, will Himself perfect, confirm, strengthen and establish you (NAS).

As the Lord washes you, He will give you the desire to re-establish and strengthen the relationship with your husband. You might begin this process by:

deciding to start right now;
examining how much you really know about your mate;
confessing your shortcomings to him; and
committing to renew the feelings you once had for your mate.

Then you can begin welcoming him into the furthest reaches of your heart.

The Welcoming Heart

Can you give him a welcoming heart? Can you say, "I'm well. Come on in."

What is "wellness"? It begins when we put our priorities in line. Let me illustrate.

Don and I were on a date. When we returned to my

house after dinner, he opened the door for me. My house had been ransacked by a burglar!

We searched through the mess trying to figure out what the thieves had taken. All my jewelry and my camera and many other "things" were gone.

Ironically, I had spent two days in court arguing with my ex-husband over my rights to those items. Now I had lost them in an instant.

Because of this experience, Matthew 6:19-21 has new impact for me:

> Do not lay up for yourselves treasures upon earth, where moth and rust destroy, and where thieves break in and steal. But lay up for yourselves treasures in heaven, where neither moth nor rust destroys, and where thieves do not break in and steal; for where your treasure is, there will your heart be also (NAS).

I had read this verse before the burglary, but it became real for me after that night. I decided that when I had more jewelry than I could wear at one time, it was too much. I realized that people were more important than things.

Also, as the Lord has become a greater part of my daily life, my heart has become more welcoming. I have learned to become transparent. I am not afraid of sharing "me" with others, even though I might be hurt.

When I went through my divorce, I felt so empty because I had no one to love. I wanted to give to another person. But I slowly closed myself to protect my feelings. By becoming more transparent, I have recaptured my longing to give and not be afraid of the results. I don't want to sound too much like Pollyanna about this. Many days I feel drained emotionally and want someone to give to me. When this happens, I realize I haven't been in touch with the Lord as often as I need to be. Getting back to Bible study and prayer helps me refocus and quit feeling like "poor me."

A sense of humor plays a valuable part in developing a welcoming heart. The ability to laugh with others rather than at them and to laugh at yourself is critical to health and wellness.

In fact, the positive effects of humor on our bodies has received increasing attention from medical researchers. Some hospitals have created "humor rooms." We still use the phrase "good humor" to describe a person who is smiling, feeling well and laughs readily.

Proverbs 31:25,26 encourages godly women to be lighthearted:

> Strength and dignity are her clothing, and she smiles at the future. She opens her mouth in wisdom and the teaching of kindness is on her tongue (NAS).

The ability to laugh at your circumstances and at your future will help you establish relationships, relieve anxiety, reduce stress, release anger and facilitate learning. My welcoming heart can laugh at uncomfortable situations and is open to the lessons the Lord wants to teach me, including how to live joyfully with Don.

In my desire to become more transparent, I discovered a need for closeness. Immediately preceding and during my divorce, the loneliness and isolation I felt hindered intimacy. There have been times during each of my marriages that I have been lonely, but not to the degree I experienced during the years I was divorced. I felt I had no one in the world I could depend on. My parents, brother, sister and son loved and supported me, but that did not fill the void. The Lord became my closest friend as I moved out of the wounded heart phase and through the willing phase. He became very real to me as I moved into the washed phase.

In the welcoming stage, I discovered my need for intimacy. As I became more intimate with the Lord, I desired more with Don. My spiritual relationship was the healing power that brought me to the place where I could open myself to others, especially Don.

If you are feeling some of the same things I did, I encourage you to lead the way toward intimacy. A welcoming heart does not require that your husband feel the same way. You can inspire him to become more vulnerable and intimate.

Seek wellness from God. Allow time for healing and invite your husband to share your inner person. You will find the "treasures" of relationships, first with your heavenly Father, then with your husband, family and friends. Your closets will be brimming with joy and happiness and the satisfaction that comes from growing in wholeness and peace.

MAKING OF A MIRACLE

Kidnap your husband for a weekend retreat or a romantic candlelight dinner. Share with him what the Lord has revealed to you about the *closets of your heart*. If you have difficulty expressing yourself to him, write him a letter and give it to him during your romantic evening or weekend.

Blend for the week of _____

I give my life to Christ, so I can give my heart to you.

*Husbands and wives are fellow heirs of the grace
of life. Honor each other so that your
prayers may not be hindered.*
(1 Peter 3:7, personal paraphrase)

*Blessings for the week of*_____

16

Man to Man: A Marriage That Sizzles

Don

Remember the chase? You saw this lovely woman who piqued your interest. What first caught your attention? Was it her luxurious hair, her confident walk or the elegant way she dressed?

The first thing that attracted me to LaDean was her translucent green eyes and the delicate softness of her skin. I also noticed her gentle, tender spirit. I would "haul hay" for one of her kisses. They are the world's greatest!

Soon the capture is done, and you take home the girl of your dreams. But suddenly you realize that you didn't win an obedient pet. The sweet and giving person you thought you married sometimes exhibits the disposition of Queen Kong. You don't understand her anymore. Contention and arguments arise, draining the thrill and excitement from your relationship.

How will you ever recover the closeness you once had?

Relationship Revolution

Remember how quickly the "honeymoon" period was over? As a single, you fell in love with your mate's strengths, but after the wedding ceremony, you went home to live with her weaknesses.

Now, men, before you get too noisy saying, "Yeah, yeah," remember that the same thing happened to her. Suddenly, both of you find traits in the other that irritate and frustrate. In addition, family routines, hectic schedules and career demands lock you into habits that drain the energy from your relationship. In a blended family, this is compounded by the presence of two-legged beasties who suddenly are not for this union like they were before the wedding.

How can you bring the sizzle back into your marriage?

In my experience of leading workshops and working with blended husbands, I have uncovered seven principles that will help revolutionize your relationship:

1. Choose to Be a Loving Person

Most of us men grew up on movies starring John Wayne and Kirk Douglas. For twenty to twenty-five years, we observed a distorted view of how a "real man" wins a woman.

We are born with a chauvinistic nature that wants our own way. But this attitude saps a relationship of fun, excitement and power.

If you love your wife only when it is convenient or just when she can fulfill your needs, you don't love her according to the scriptural pattern. The Book of Ephesians tells us to love our wives as Christ loved the church (5:25). This agape love means devoting yourself to her in spite of circumstances and regardless of her attitude. Agape love sacrifices and provides the only lasting romance in marriage.

Agape love goes beyond sex and friendship. It flows from the soul. It is based on God's love and on the example of Christ's choice to die on the cross for us.

When you feel your feelings waning, remind yourself that love is a choice. Do the things a lover does. What did you do to win her in the first place? Did you send cards or flowers? Did you take walks in the park together? Ask God to help you commit yourself to your partner despite your emotions. God will do His part in restoring your love for your wife. Our part is to pray and fill our minds with loving thoughts.

There is nothing like conflict in the home to discourage any loving actions on our part. Many men prefer to retreat from conflict. They hide in their work, sports, hobbies or television. One of the strongest statements you can make about your commitment to love your wife is to turn the TV off or to give up some golf time.

Keep in mind that you are responsible for your attitudes and actions, and not for her responses. It may take time to prove to her that you are for real.

Do you choose to love her in your thought life? Because of our human nature, our imagination can be our greatest ally or our worst enemy. Are you in the habit of daydreaming about other lives and other situations? The only woman you need to fantasize about is your wife, so choose to replay in your mind the best times you have experienced as a couple. Make those images the object of your affection.

I once heard a story about a rich, clever trader in the South Pacific who married a "plain-looking" wife. His friends laughed because he paid eight cows for her. "You haven't traded wisely," they sneered. "Look at the many beautiful women you could have had."

The trader took his wife to another island to live.

Some time later, an outsider visited the man. The trader treated his guest graciously and kindly.

"And how is your wife?" the outsider asked, curious about the islander's selection of a plain-looking woman.

The trader invited his wife in to meet the visitor. Amazed, he saw one of the most beautiful women he had seen on any of the islands. She stood tall and proud, obviously in love.

After she left, the trader explained, "When I looked for a wife, I didn't like it when my friends bragged about how much a woman cost. So I treated my wife as if she were worth more than all the others. Soon her inside beauty began to shine on the outside."

A woman whose husband treats her like the most important person on earth develops a radiance—an inner beauty which comes from knowing that she is loved completely and freely. Her lovely qualities are encouraged, and she returns that love in a similar way. Such unconditional love enables intimacy to grow in the midst of the humdrum or the crises of life.

Men, if we are honest with ourselves, we'll admit that we want to be loved for our inner person, too. Beauty, desire, hormones and companionship are added attractions, like frosting on the cake, but these come and go. The real foundation for love is to know the heart and soul of your partner, not just her body. If we model this, our wives will love us for our inner selves as well. And our home becomes a model for the way Christ cares for His own. Choosing to love glorifies God.

2. Understand the Differences in Focus Between Women and Men

Women usually have a more detailed, immediate focus that spirals inward to the object of their concern. Men tend to have a general, long-range and broader scope of interest. How many times have you planned a yearly budget and your wife asks, "But what about that bill due tomorrow? And you know Jimmy's eyeglasses need to be fixed."

Since men tend to forget about detailed essentials when everything seems to be going well, a wise husband will listen to his wife when she points out a specific need. Often LaDean brings to my attention a potential problem that I have not recognized. When I appreciate her contribution, I make her conscious of her value and worth. This begins the process in my mind of making her needs as important to me as my needs are. It also provides less room for manipulative habits that arise when one partner doesn't listen to the other.

3. Understand the Role of Sin in This Relationship

A husband's greatest sin against his wife is pride. It is really sin against God. The Lord declares, "Pride and arrogance . . . I hate" (Proverbs 8:13, NAS). We also read, " 'Behold, I am against you, O arrogant one,' declares the Lord GOD of hosts" (Jeremiah 50:31, NAS).

A man who automatically says no to every suggestion or desire of his wife is operating out of pride. I know that most of the turmoil in my life has this origin. Sadly, sometimes I have to experience emotional and spiritual pain before I am reminded that my pride is my worst enemy.

When I humble myself before God, He restores my spirit, and my relationship with LaDean is once more open and loving. If I admit my failures to her, she feels safer with me.

4. Provide Spiritual Leadership

LaDean needs to see where I am going in my relationship with the Lord. A lack of desire in me to seek the Lord causes insecurity in her. My submission to God gives her security and freedom to be radiant. (Read this again—it really works.)

Providing spiritual leadership means following through with my convictions. What I say must be how I live. She must see me cleansing myself of anger, bitterness and pride and replacing those killers with love and transparency.

Spiritual leadership also involves opening my heart to her in prayer and sharing. This communicates my dependence on God.

I "kidnapped" LaDean one weekend, and we drove up to the hill country of Texas where I grew up. We had been married five years.

As we passed through familiar scenery, I began to share some deep things with her. I told her about my childhood and teenage years. I related some of the hurtful things I had done to people as well as my wrongful thoughts. I poured out the secrets of my heart to her.

She just listened, her eyes mirroring my pain. She never passed judgment or appeared shocked at what I was telling her.

We drove for a couple of hours. I wept and confessed; she listened. For the first time, I began trusting her with my weaknesses and depending on God for her love for me. That day, she became my closest friend, both by what I revealed of myself and how she received it.

As a result of my transparency, LaDean began praying for me daily. I also gained freedom to do the same for her and to not fear praying with her about anything. We began going to the Lord together, asking Him to improve specific areas of our relationship.

You may not feel comfortable in revealing yourself so much at one time like I did. But whether you share a bit at a time or all at once, open yourself to your wife. Your transparency will help her respond by being open with you.

5. Make Her Feel Special

Sometimes the atmosphere in a marriage can be cold as icicles. If this is the situation in your home, have hope! By treating your wife special, you can be the warmth that melts the ice.

Make her your best friend. A wife should know and feel that she is more a part of you than your buddies at work. Do things for her that are not natural for you to show your love for her. For instance, send her flowers just to say, "You are special." LaDean teaches Office Administration Systems. One year on Secretary's Day, I sent a bouquet to her as teacher of office administrators. That was some of the best money I ever spent.

Kidnapping is another wonderful way to show her how important she is. Walk into the house some Friday evening and announce, "If you want to wear any clothes this weekend, you'd better get them into a suitcase quick."

Of course, you have already made arrangements for the kids for the next few days. (You could swap babysitting with another couple.) And you have made reservations at a nearby hotel. (Most hotels have a getaway package which will give both of you a chance to refocus on each other for twenty-four or thirty-six hours.) Then whisk her off to a weekend of fun and sharing.

Another way to treat her special is to make her feel she is the most important part of your day. Convey to her that she fulfills your life. Let her know that you think about her when you are apart.

Whenever she comes to mind, pray for her. That's one of God's ways of keeping your love alive.

Do little things that she appreciates. I open doors for my wife, seat her at the table, help her into the car even when she drives. Find someone to watch the kids and take her out to a movie. A lunch at McDonald's can be a big thing when she has a hectic schedule. Telephone her during the middle of the day just to say, "I love you."

Make your wife feel a vital part of your life.

Only once did LaDean complain about the amount of time I spent on coaching. That started a heated argument. I did my best to make her feel guilty about her attitude. Then the Lord spoke to my inner person: *Don, the real problem is you. LaDean does not feel she is a part of your life.*

Suddenly, I realized that I was keeping all my coaching problems to myself. And she knew it. I began to share my failures and fears with her, and her nurturing spirit supported me.

Now whenever LaDean tries to control my life, I see a red flag waving a signal that she doesn't feel important to me. I look at myself first to determine where I have shut her out. Then I open myself to sharing again.

I encourage you to consciously plan to treat your wife special. Unless you set aside time for her, daily pressures will rob you of opportunities to let her know how much you care.

6. Understand the Role of Respect

If you really want your wife to be an intimate part of your life, don't be discouraged if it takes her time to believe you love her. You may have lived for months or years cultivating wrong attitudes. Be tough enough to allow the same amount or even more time to achieve peace and restoration.

Treating her with respect accelerates this building process. This means approaching her with humility. I desire her to praise me for success, but because she is created as a nurturing person her desire is to see the vulnerability in me. This means being honest about myself. I will win her love more by sharing my inner fears and failures than by reporting my successes. By being vulnerable before her I allow her to become a part of the solution. This becomes marriage cement.

However, I must refrain from using "poor me" as an excuse to get my way or manipulate her. This is an important principle to understand since the benefits are so very great and the effects of misuse are so devastating. Keep in mind one of the most powerful ingredients in this process is a sense of humor. Being able to laugh at ourselves can be the open door to understanding and acceptance.

Consider her opinions valuable and her contribution to your life as extremely important. She adds immeasurably to your life.

Treat her with the dignity that every woman desires. Both in your thoughts and with your words, build up her image by emphasizing her wholesome virtues. Do not reflect on her weaknesses or call attention to them in front of the children.

Respect your wife by learning how to argue fairly. LaDean and I are both strong-willed and tough, so we have to practice disagreeing without chaos. We no longer have World War III over every conflict. It's my responsibility to speak gently and stem harsh or destructive words.

Learning to focus on the positives and not the negatives is changing our marriage into a more harmonious relationship. We find that as we seek more and more to be "in Christ," we are better able to accept and respect each other's differences. We both feel that perhaps we could have saved our previous marriages had we known then what we know now about relationships and ourselves. Remember, divorce rarely solves problems; it always creates them.

7. Understand the Bonding of Sex

Sexual love is life's greatest tension reliever. But

how can you make your physical relationship so good that your wife feels fulfilled and excited?

Sexual intimacy thrives in spiritual freedom. God is pleased when His children claim the joy He created for a physical relationship within marriage. This closeness is accentuated as we use the other six qualities mentioned earlier to build intimacy. Let me explain.

First, choosing to be a loving person regardless of circumstances stabilizes my relationship with LaDean. This allows me to meet her sexual needs more consistently and not just when things are going smoothly between us. When sex is out of real love, my wife can develop fulfilled radiance.

In turn, physical love relaxes our emotions. Sometimes LaDean and I begin tough discussions with sexual intimacy. Our closeness helps us focus on the real issues and not just the symptoms.

Second, understanding the difference between women and men helps me respond to her appropriately. Women enjoy tenderness. They are more emotional while men are more visual. Knowing these dissimilarities allows me to fulfill her completely, and she can do the same for me.

Third, dealing with sin in my life breaks down barriers between us. If I act haughty, angry or mistreat our relationship in any way, our intimacy is marred. But through confession, both to the Lord and to my wife, I build bridges that lead to a more satisfying physical union as well.

I would especially like to encourage you to take control of lustful thoughts. When you start to think of something or someone you shouldn't, immediately picture your wife's inner and outer beauty. Make her the desire of your heart, and you will find that your sexual needs are more thoroughly fulfilled than you could ever imagine.

Fourth, my spiritual leadership enables her to trust

me with her most private moments. As I become more Christ-like in spirit, she will be more attracted to me emotionally and physically.

Fifth, making her feel special involves understanding the vulnerability of our egos in God's most unique intimacy. God designed a husband and wife to fulfill each other's needs. When I make my wife feel she completes me sexually, I am reminded that sex is not for my needs only.

Sixth, respect helps a husband bring out his wife's capacity for physical love. If he continues to praise her and give her "good strokes," her self-image is strengthened. She feels more loveable and responds to his affection. This naturally leads to a healthier sexual relationship.

I encourage you to try these suggestions. You will embark on one of the greatest experiences in your life, and you will see a revolution in your relationship. The sparkle and thrill of an intimacy that sizzles will flourish in your home.

MAKING OF A MIRACLE

The making of this miracle will require closeness. You'll want to find time alone as a couple. Begin with prayer to open your hearts before each other and before God. Next, share with each other an inner fear you have never expressed before. This will be tough, but have faith in your mate and in God. The listening mate should refrain from judgments or opinions. Just accept what is said as a valid feeling. Allow God and your love for each other to bind you together in this special moment.

While you're close, share with your mate a quality of hers you really adore. It can be physical, emotional or spiritual. Be willing to share deep feelings. Refer to the Blend Card, and fill the Blessing Card with all the special intimate feelings you have. Y'all are in for a great experience.

Blend for the week of _____

I will grow with you in all that you achieve.

Let no unwholesome word proceed from your mouth,
but only such a word as is good for edification . . .
that it may give grace to those who hear.
(Ephesians 4:29, NAS)

*Blessings for the week of*_____

17

Expect a Miracle!

Don

By now, you have taken a good look at the struggles LaDean and I have experienced on our journey to harmony. You have seen some of our weaknesses and our strengths and how these have affected our relationship.

In opening our lives to you, we have not tried to paint a super-rosy picture of remarriage. It is the hardest work we have ever done. We still struggle with selfishness, unkindness and insensitivity. Both of us have shed many tears and spent many sleepless nights working out the principles we have shared with you.

Any marriage, whether the first or second or third one, is a process of change and releasing in order to gain the precious treasure of intimacy. But we can attest that the journey gets better as we go along. There is great joy to be had. Now we come home after a long day to an atmosphere of contentment. When one of us has a special need, the other gives support. And you should see the fun we have on trips these days!

Part of charting your course is deciding where you are comfortable as a couple and challenging yourself to go one step deeper into sharing with each other. If your spouse feels strongly about a lack of closeness in a particular area, work to fulfill that need. When we know that our mate is there for us, we feel more confident about trusting them with our feelings and needs. Remain constant in your quest for more closeness without pushing too quickly.

If your spouse is not excited about this journey, continue to show your enthusiasm. Be as transparent as you can and treat your mate like a special guest in your home. You will discover that respect will bring sparkle and strength to your relationship.

Begin the Journey

If anyone had told us years ago that we would be helping other couples build "miracle marriages," we would have laughed. Our relationship looked hopeless.

But God took two of the most unlikely—but willing—people and welded a bond that has given us immeasurable pleasure and security. We turned our hurtful pasts and damaged relationships into a marriage that glorifies Him. And every day our love grows deeper and more exciting. That's not normal. That's a miracle.

We encourage you to experience this, too. Diligently apply the skills and principles we have shared in this book. If you have committed your marriage to the Lord and given yourself unreservedly to your partner, you have already begun the thrilling adventure. Building a strong marital bond will keep you on the road together and give you the serenity of a stable relationship.

Your forgiving spirit will keep your love fresh and growing. Accepting your partner's personality and applying good communication skills will allow sensitivity and caring to blossom.

We urge you to claim victory over the danger zones in your marriage by using biblical tools for spiritual warfare. Through prayer and a deeper knowledge of

God's Word, protect your family from evil and build a vital spiritual atmosphere in your home. Confront the conflicts of the money crunch by wisely handling your finances, and foster a selfless spirit in yourself and in your loved ones through cheerful giving.

An exciting part of building a close relationship is seeing the beneficial effects on your children. Through the steps to power parenting, help build positive values and esteem in their lives. The joy and agreement they see in the two of you will open their hearts to share your closeness.

The treasure of a full, rich relationship is at your fingertips. Begin right where you are to reconstruct your marriage. And expect a miracle! The blessings of God and the thrill of a lifetime will be the rewards of your journey to intimacy and harmony.

MAKING OF A MIRACLE

To reaffirm your commitment to each other and to your family, we suggest that you and your mate renew your wedding vows. Individually write down what you want to pledge to your partner. Then come together as a couple to commit your vows to each other.

You can choose to renew your vows privately or with the family present. Some couples prefer private intimacy; others have asked their pastor to lead this commitment time. Including the children gives them an opportunity to witness your verbal commitment to each other. We suggest a chapel or romantic setting in which to exchange your vows.

Consider this ceremony your new beginning, a chance to start over. After completing your vows, give a reception to celebrate with family and friends. Let your children play a major role in planning and participating in the fun. This may be the beginning of family unity. We believe that as a couple bonds, the family blends.

Of course, after every wedding and reception comes

a honeymoon. This doesn't have to be an elaborate excursion. Perhaps someone would keep the kids for a night or a weekend. Or you could plan a special evening at home as a couple. Allow the older children to care for the younger ones while the two of you spend time together.

Blend for the week of _____

In my hands I hold today.
In my dreams I hold tomorrow.
In my faith I hold eternity.

Having started the ball rolling so enthusiastically, you should carry this project through to completion just as gladly, giving whatever you can out of whatever you have. Let your enthusiastic idea at the start be equalled by your realistic action now. (2 Corinthians 8:11, TLB)

*Blessings for the week of*_____

Don and LaDean Houck are available to conduct marriage and family workshops for your group. They can be contacted at:

> Blended Blessings
> 4101 Green Oaks Blvd. W., Suite 207
> Arlington, TX 76016

Would You Like to Know God Personally?

The following four principles[1] will help you discover how to know God personally and experience the abundant life He promised.

1. *God loves you, and created you to know Him personally.*

While the Bible is filled with assurances of God's love, perhaps the most telling verse is John 3:16:

> For God so loved the world, that He gave His only begotten Son, that whoever believes in Him should not perish, but have eternal life (NAS).

God not only loves each of us enough to give His only Son for us, He desires that we come to know Him personally:

> Now this is eternal life; that they may know you, the only true God, and Jesus Christ, whom you have sent (John 17:3, NIV).

What, then, prevents us from knowing God personally?

2. *Men and women are sinful and separated from God, so we cannot know Him personally or experience His love.*

We were all created to have fellowship with God; but, because of mankind's stubborn self-will, we chose to go our own independent way and fellowship with God was broken. This self-will, characterized by an attitude of active rebellion or passive indifference, is evidence of what the Bible calls sin.

> For all have sinned and fall short of the glory of God (Romans 3:23, NAS).

The Bible also tells us that "the wages of sin is death" (Romans 6:23), or spiritual separation from God. When we are in this state, a great gulf separates us from God, because He cannot tolerate sin. People often try to bridge the gulf by doing good works or devoting themselves to religious or New Age practices, but the Bible clearly teaches that there is only one way to bridge this gulf . . .

3. *Jesus Christ is God's ONLY provision for our sin. Through Him alone we can know God personally and experience His love.*

God's Word records three important facts to verify this principle: (1) Jesus Christ died in our place; (2) He rose from the dead; and (3) He is our only way to God:

> But God demonstrates His own love toward us, in that while we were yet sinners, Christ died for us (Romans 5:8, NAS).

Christ died for our sins . . . He was buried . . . He was raised on the third day according to the Scriptures . . . He appeared to Peter, then to the twelve. After that He appeared to more than five hundred . . . (1 Corinthians 15:3-6, NAS).

Jesus said to him, "I am the way, and the truth, and the life; no one comes to the Father, but through Me" (John 14:6, NAS).

Thus, God has taken the loving initiative to bridge the gulf which separates us from Him by sending His Son, Jesus Christ, to die on the cross in our place to pay the penalty for our sin. But it is not enough just to know these truths . . .

4. *We must individually receive Jesus Christ as Savior and Lord; then we can know God personally and experience His love.*

John 1:12 records:

But as many as received Him, to them He gave the right to become children of God, even to those who believe in His name (NAS).

What does it mean to "receive Christ"? The Scriptures tell us that we receive Christ through faith—not through "good works" or religious endeavors:

For by grace you have been saved through faith; and that not of yourselves, it is the gift of God; not as a result of works, that no one should boast (Ephesians 2:8,9, NAS).

We're also told that receiving Christ means to personally invite Him into our lives:

(Christ is speaking): Behold, I stand at the door

and knock; if anyone hears My voice and opens the door, I will come in to him (Revelation 3:20, NAS).

Thus, receiving Christ involves turning to God from self . . . and trusting Christ to come into our lives to forgive our sins and to make us the kind of people He wants us to be.

If you are not sure whether you have ever committed your life to Jesus Christ, I encourage you to do so—today! Here is a suggested prayer which has helped millions of men and women around the world express faith in Him and invite Him into their lives:

Lord Jesus, I want to know You personally. Thank You for dying on the cross for my sins. I open the door of my life and receive You as my Savior and Lord. Thank You for forgiving my sins and giving me eternal life. Take control of the throne of my life. Make me the kind of person You want me to be.

If this prayer expresses the desire of your heart, why not pray it now? If you mean it sincerely, Jesus Christ will come into your life, just as He promised in Revelation 3:20. He keeps His promises! And there is another key promise I suggest you write indelibly in your mind:

And the witness is this, that God has given us eternal life, and this life is in His Son. He who has the Son has the life; he who does not have the Son of God does not have the life. These things I have written to you who believe in the name of the Son of God, in order that you may **know** that you have eternal life (1 John 5:11-13, NAS).

That's right—the man or woman who personally receives Christ as Savior and Lord is assured of everlasting life with Him in heaven. So, in summary, when you received Christ by faith, as an act of your will, many wonderful things happened including the following:

1. Christ came into your life (Revelation 3:20 and Colossians 1:27).

2. Your sins were forgiven (Colossians 1:14).

3. You became a child of God (John 1:12).

4. You received eternal life (John 5:24).

5. You began the great adventure for which God created you (John 10:10; 1 Thessalonians 5:18).

Steven Pogue has written an excellent book designed to help you make the most of your new life in Christ. The title is *The First Year of Your Christian Life* and it is available in Christian bookstores everywhere. To order directly from the publisher, please call 1-800-950-4457.

Notes

Chapter 1

1. As reported during the September 1990 TV program, "Real Life With Jane Pauley."

Chapter 7

1. The "Personality Profile" was created by Fred Littauer and may not be reproduced without permission. Additional copies can be ordered from CLASS Speakers, 1645 S. Rancho Santa Fe, #102, San Marcos, CA 92069; (619) 471-0233.

Appendix A

1. The four principles are adapted from *Would You Like to Know God Personally?* (Here's Life Publishers, 1987). Used by permission.

Making Good
Marriages Better

Quantity   Total

Managing Stress In Marriage by Bill and Vonette $ _____
Bright. A delightfully candid book with practical help for
busy couples who experience added stress from the
hectic pace of dual careers or ministry involvement.
ISBN 0-89840-272-7/$8.99

Building Your Mate's Self-Esteem by Dennis and $ _____
Barbara Rainey. Ten essential building blocks for
strengthening your mate's self-esteem, with creative
ideas for immediate results. ISBN 0-89840-105-4/$8.99

What Makes a Marriage Last? by William L. Coleman. $ _____
A survey of 1000 people reveals the key steps every
couple can take to build an exciting and enduring
relationship. ISBN 0-89840-293-X/$7.99

When Two Walk Together by Richard and Mary $ _____
Strauss. Join Richard and Mary Strauss in their
discovery of intimacy through better communication.
ISBN 0-89840-216-6/$7.99

**Your Christian bookseller should have these products in stock.
Please check with him before using this "Shop by Mail" form.**

Send completed order form to: **HERE'S LIFE PUBLISHERS, INC.**
                              P. O. Box 1576
                              San Bernardino, CA 92402-1576

Name _____

Address _____

City _____ State _____ Zip _____

❑ Payment enclosed (check or money order only) ❑ Visa ❑ Mastercard # _____ Expiration Date _____ Signature _____	**ORDER TOTAL** $ _____ **SHIPPING and HANDLING** $ _____ ($1.50 for one item, $0.50 for each additional. Do not exceed $4.00.) **APPLICABLE SALES TAX (CA 7%)** $ _____ **TOTAL DUE** $ _____

**For faster service,
call toll free:
1-800-950-4457**

Please allow 2 to 4 weeks for delivery.
Prices subject to change without notice.

Building Stronger Families

Quantity		Total
‾‾‾‾	**"Mom and Dad Don't Live Together Anymore"** by Gary and Angela Hunt. A book for children of divorce, from middle school to high school age students. Each chapter addresses a specific need the child may have developed as a result of divorce in his or her family. ISBN 0-89840-199-2/$5.99	$ ‾‾‾‾
‾‾‾‾	**Helping Your Kids Handle Stress** by H. Norman Wright. Counselor Norm Wright helps parents learn to recognize the symptoms of stress in children and how to reduce its harmful effects. ISBN 0-89840-271-9/$7.99	$ ‾‾‾‾
‾‾‾‾	**The Dad Difference** by Josh McDowell and Dr. Norm Wakefield. A discussion of the crucial roles fathers play in shaping the values and morals of their children. ISBN 0-89840-252-2/$8.99	$ ‾‾‾‾
‾‾‾‾	**Family Fitness Fun** by Charles Kuntzleman. Help your loved ones build lifetime habits for good health. Includes more than 180 activities! ISBN 0-89840-279-4/$9.99	$ ‾‾‾‾

Your Christian bookseller should have these products in stock. Please check with him before using this "Shop by Mail" form.

Send completed order form to: **HERE'S LIFE PUBLISHERS, INC.**
P. O. Box 1576
San Bernardino, CA 92402-1576

Name ‾‾‾‾‾‾‾‾‾‾‾‾‾‾‾‾‾‾‾‾‾‾‾‾‾‾‾‾‾‾‾‾‾‾‾‾‾‾

Address ‾‾‾‾‾‾‾‾‾‾‾‾‾‾‾‾‾‾‾‾‾‾‾‾‾‾‾‾‾‾‾‾‾‾

City ‾‾‾‾‾‾‾‾‾‾‾‾‾ State ‾‾‾‾‾‾ Zip ‾‾‾‾‾‾

❑ Payment enclosed
   (check or money order only)
❑ Visa   ❑ Mastercard
#‾‾‾‾‾‾‾‾‾‾‾‾‾‾‾‾‾‾‾‾
Expiration Date ‾‾‾‾‾‾‾‾
Signature ‾‾‾‾‾‾‾‾‾‾‾‾‾‾‾

For faster service, call toll free: 1-800-950-4457

ORDER TOTAL	$ ‾‾‾
SHIPPING and HANDLING ($1.50 for one item, $0.50 for each additional. Do not exceed $4.00.)	$ ‾‾‾
APPLICABLE SALES TAX (CA 7%)	$ ‾‾‾
TOTAL DUE	$ ‾‾‾

Please allow 2 to 4 weeks for delivery.
Prices subject to change without notice.